MOTORCYCLE 101

By Dave Preston

Mixed *MEDIA*
2226 Eastlake Avenue, Suite 69
Seattle, WA 98102
www.mm411.com

©2003 by Dave Preston

All rights reserved. This book may not be duplicated or transmitted in any form by way of photocopying, recording, mechanical or electronic copying, or any otherwise means without the written consent of the publisher. The author and publisher assume no liability for any errors or omissions that may exist and the damages that may result from the use of this information.

Disclaimer: Both the author and the publisher of Motorcycle 101 disclaim any and all responsibility for the incursion of, personal or other than personal, liabilities and risks from the application or direct or indirect use of any of the contents of this book.

MIXED *MEDIA* PRODUCTION TEAM

Publisher
Tom Mehren

Editing
Danielle Scoggins
Tamara Timmons

Layout & Design
Tom Mehren
Tamara Timmons
Mike Hew

Photography
Tom Mehren

Printing
Gorham Printing, WA

Table of Contents

1. THINKING ABOUT A MOTORCYCLE? 1
2. ACCESSORIES 11
3. HOW TO BUY HELMETS 13
4. HOW TO BUY GLOVES 23
5. HOW TO BUY JACKETS AND RAIN GEAR 29
6. HOW TO BUY PANTS AND BOOTS 39
7. HOW TO BUY FOOTWEAR 45
8. BUYING YOUR MOTORCYCLE 51
9. BUYING INSURANCE 65
10. YOUR EVERYDAY RIDING SYSTEM 69
11. THE DEVELOPMENTAL STAGES OF A MOTORCYCLIST 75
12. GIVING A FRIEND A FIRST RIDE 83
13. COMMUTING TO WORK 91
14. TEN TIPS 97
15. HOW TO TALK MOTORCYCLE 105
16. CLEANLINESS IS NEXT TO GODLINESS 117
17. THE LONG TRIP 121
18. CAVEATS 129

Motorcycle 101 - Introduction

I had my first experience on a motorcycle at fifteen, as a passenger, one fine summer day in 1962. "Epiphany" is not too strong a word to use, as just a few minutes changed my life forever. A friend of my older brother's showed me the road that wove around the lake in front of our suburban Minneapolis home and meandered back to a dam on Minnehaha Creek. Unlike many who use such rides to impress (terrify) the novice, Richard was serious about motorcycles, and took the time to explain to me how to lean (only as far as he did) and how to relax, before we left. He rode briskly and with skill, but in a manner that emphasized the magic carpet qualities of a motorcycle without encroaching on my sense of personal safety.

I wanted one. Pure and simple. It was obvious to me, as few things before or since, that riding a motorcycle was what I was meant to do. There was no doubt, no discussion, and nothing to ponder – this was a done deal.

Oddly enough, my parents did not share my epiphany, and greeted my pronouncement that I "needed" a motorcycle with the same nonchalant and loving attention they gave to my lectures to Dad on why a new Corvette would make a great commuter car for him. (I was right about that as well, but that's another book) What followed was five years of enforced study, brought about by economic and parental factors beyond my control.

This was actually beneficial, as I used the time to read every scrap of information I could find on motorcycles, listen to anyone talking about motorcycles, gaze with longing through the windows of any store selling motorcycles, and study with great intent the 250 Honda Street Scramblers that the "cool" kids got to ride. I learned a lot, and loved the homework.

At the ripe old age of 20, I finally got to buy my first motorcycle, a pristine little blue and white Yamaha YDS3. The first owner was selling because a near crash had scared him. Sadly, the only reason my parents consented was that Mother was dying of cancer at a relatively young age, and their theories of risk and danger had been trashed forever. They also, of course, had concerns of a larger nature.

My first ride came right after I paid the $400 for the bike and the owner gave me the keys. I learned how to ride it on the way home. I looked in the rear view mirror at my Dad's laughing face as he followed me. I had killed the engine at the 5th consecutive intersection, and I was sweating bullets. I wondered how a sober-sided engineer could rationalize allowing his son to learn to ride in public traffic. True – there was a lot less traffic then.

And so, the title comes from that sepia-tinted era of late high-school and early college in my life when EVERYTHING was a course called 101. Motorcycles have taught me more than all of the other courses I took – including seven years of college. Best of all, I'm still learning, and the topic is so vast and of such fascination and depth for me that I am still enrolled in Motorcycle 101. I do not plan to graduate – ever.

My thanks to Susan, who has always believed I can do any whacky thing I dream up, and also to Richard - for that first ride. Thanks to Jim Boltz and everyone at Cycle Barn for helping out with the photos in this book.

CHAPTER ONE

Thinking About a Motorcycle?

You've seen them on a winding road on a sun-dappled day, swooping back and forth around corners, or motoring down a straight. You've noticed couples cruising on the Interstate, with intercoms connecting their matching helmets. You've seen groups of the guys 'hanging out" on weekends with their two- wheeled friends, and noticed that some of the guys ...are gals! Maybe you remember youthful adventures with motorcycles, before you "grew up" and became "mature." Or, you're a young person attracted to the speed, the cornering, and the thrill motorcycling appears to offer. It all looks like such epic fun. Know what? It is.

Two-wheeled vehicles have attracted your attention, and you're contemplating a plunge into a fascinating world. What to buy? What to avoid? What other costs may be involved? What will Mom think? Information, ideas, and hours of thought are your friends, and this book is meant to help you form your own opinions and make the right decisions... for you.

WELCOME TO MOTORCYCLING!

Motorcycles have brought constant joy to my life for over 40 years, and may they bring happiness, adventure, and education to you as well. But first, let's make sure we understand a central truth: Motorcycles are a very serious hobby. They are expensive, in both time and money. They are dangerous, and while various types of dangers can be reduced and/or eliminated, others cannot be controlled.

INITIAL MUSTS

1. You **MUST** take a Motorcycle Safety Foundation course, preferably before you purchase any motorcycle. It will save you time and money, and make you a much better rider. Many long-term motorcyclists are cavorting around with all kinds of bad habits they do not know they possess, habits an MSF course will keep you from ever attaining.

2. You **MUST** wear a helmet... always. It can be hot and sticky in summer, and so is what's inside your head. The human skull was never designed for the impact of even a minor fall, and the miracles of modern medicine can fix almost every area of your body, except the head.

3. You <u>MUST</u> make a commitment to not drinking alcohol, EVER, before a ride. I had one beer, once, and I was terrified that I could discern the difference, albeit slight. A motorcycle demands the full and concentrated use of your head, hands, and feet - all at once, and at all times. You simply cannot afford to allow any decrease in your performance, ever.

I make a conscious effort to use my helmet as a switch: when I pull it on any and all other concerns about money, job, relationships, world peace... all are blocked out. Nothing is to be processed now but the operation of the motorcycle. If you can learn this trick it's actually quite restful, as it gives your brain a break from the motley concerns of the day. Try memorizing and repeating this simple sentence: "When the helmet drops, the bullshit stops." A bit crude, but very effective if repeated every time you pull a helmet onto your head.

Now then, assuming you're still there...

WHAT KIND OF MOTORCYCLE?

This book focuses primarily on street bikes, and they can be classified by displacement and/or usage category. There are 600s, 750s, 1000s, and so forth, measured in the cubic centimeter displacement of the engine, and there are also Cruisers, Power Cruisers, Sports Bikes, Touring Bikes, Standards, and Naked Street bikes. Occasionally you may come across a motorcycle that does not fall into a handy displacement slot. It may be the harbinger of a new usage category! It seems confusing at first, but it will all make sense in about six minutes.

Here are descriptions of the terms commonly used:

STANDARD

This is, as you might guess, a "normal" motorcycle used for almost anything. Fifty years ago, all motorcycles were "standards." They are often referred to as "UJMs" as well, for universal Japanese motorcycle... a four cylinder four stroke engine across the frame, five speeds, etc. There are also smaller motorcycles, usually twin cylinder designs. Either a twin or a UJM would be excellent for a new buyer, especially if you will be buying a used model.

SPORTBIKE

Sport bikes have been designed to bring as much of the handling, brakes, and power of road racing bikes as is practical to the world of street legal machines. In recent years, competition for sales in this market has stretched the definition of "practical." You can now purchase bikes from several manufacturers which are essentially track ready – which may or may not be a good thing. They have much lower handlebars for aerodynamics and higher foot pegs for cornering clearance, plus swoopy aerodynamic bodywork, and feature enormous performance capabilities.

For several decades, motorcycle magazines sold copies based on road tests of new bikes, and the magazine editors always tested the bikes in the most extreme circumstances possible – a race track. They did this for one reason – it sells more magazines, and selling magazines is what they are all about. They would routinely ask for more – more power, more brakes, better handling. Currently they are a bit stuck, as a few have actually put in print the numbing fact that the top bikes on offer today have "enough." In fact, with the ability to flip themselves either backwards or forwards with race-derived power and brakes, some magazines are edging toward phrases like "too much." This does NOT sell copies, so it will be interesting to follow developments in the next couple of years.

To be blunt, modern sport bikes offer a great deal more capability than most know how to use, (including me) and an impressive and tragic percentage of sport bikes are crashed at a very low mileage – a few years ago the AVERAGE was less than 10,000 miles.

Having said that, there is joy and beauty to be found in this class, and they offer a tremendous riding experience – IF the owner has the mental discipline to control his or her riding actions. The most popular class is 600cc, and I doubt you can sit on one comfortably for very long if you are older than twenty-five. As a very rough rule of butt – the bigger the engine in displacement, the more room for legs and arms and "stomach muscle." If you are of a certain age, the bold styling and graphics of many sport bikes might make you feel a little silly... but that is what sells, so what do I know? If you prefer a more monochromatic look, there are machines available – and/or custom paint jobs.

CRUISER

Like sport bikes, these have a lot of eye candy to their design. They are meant to make you look cool while cruising the burger joints or whatever. Almost all Harleys are cruisers, and all of the Japanese manufacturers make cruisers, many of which are shameless Harley clones. The riding position has the torso leaned back with the arms outstretched, which makes most of us look better but can be uncomfortable for the long distances and high speeds these bikes are not designed to sustain. Given a small windshield and some throw-over soft saddlebags, you can go touring on your cruiser, and go in style. Most of these do feature a lot of leg and arm room. Almost all are beautiful, which can be reason enough to purchase.

TOURING

As the name implies, these are motorcycles meant to be comfy on a longer ride…for several days, weeks, or even months. Tourers usually have huge barn door fairings, well- padded seats, good luggage capacity, and often CB radios, stereos, GPS systems, and even a reverse gear. The largest current models are truly gargantuan. These are often purchased by Mom and Dad couples, who cruise the Interstates in relative luxury. As a rule they are VERY heavy, due to the need to carry a lot of stuff, plus the weight of said stuff. They are not going to be the bikes of choice for the new rider, due to their weight. True, most of the road tests will describe how the weight seems to disappear at speeds above those used in a parking lot. What that means is that the new rider, and some of us who should know better, are at risk of dumping 1200 pounds of bike, rider, and passenger – in a parking lot.

NAKED STREET

Manufacturers are rushing into this segment, which has enjoyed mushrooming sales growth in the past few years. Aging sport bike riders are enthusiasts of naked street bikes because they are more comfortable and practical, (the bikes, although that is also true of the aging sport bike riders) and with the addition of saddlebags, can be used for touring quite capably. They offer very nearly the same performance "hit" of pure sport bikes, with great advantages in comfort and day to day usability. This all makes sense when you consider that sport bikes are now so highly evolved that most of their performance cannot be used on the streets, and that the buying population is aging.

ON ENGINE DISPLACEMENT HISTORY – SIZE USED TO MATTER

Almost any street motorcycle sold today has enough power, and usually far more than enough power, to do anything you will ask of it. Larger engines do tend to be housed in larger frames, so if you are large in stature you may want to shop at the "heavy end" of the market.

Although available power is no longer a real concern, it was when I started. My first 250 was nowhere near as fast as a 500, which was not as fast as a 1000, and so on. Contrast this with a modern 600cc sport bike with well over 100 hp that can easily top 140 mph. The only need for the adage of "there is no replacement for displacement" is ego. The guy with the big engine still gets more attention. If that is important to you, you may "need" the 1,000cc screamer. On the street, a 600 sport bike ridden competently is probably the fastest transportation device ever created, due to its near-perfect combination of light weight, good power, small size, and short wheelbase.

Historically, engine sizes were sorted out by cubic centimeter capacity to determine classes for racing, as in 250 cc, 500 cc, 750cc, and so on. Recent advances in both technology and marketing have made a hash of this once-rational approach, so now you have a "class" of motorcycles that is created on a manufacturing whim, and may appear and then disappear. The 900 Honda, the 1100 Kawasaki, and the Triumph 996 triple are a few examples.

In general, a larger engine will make more horsepower and use more fuel, but there are a lot of exceptions to that generalization. Suffice to say, if you are starting out, you can make your selection based on the type of motorcycle, the intended use, the appearance, and the cost. You need not be terribly concerned about the displacement, unless this is an ego thing for you!

WHAT ABOUT COSTS?

Motorcycle:

For between $2000 and $3000 you can get a lightly used and very clean motorcycle. A consideration here is that larger motorcycles are often purchased by older riders, who may end up not using them much, and then selling what was only a toy or a passing fancy for a relative pittance. Many of these motorcycles are virtually brand new, but much less expensive. By purchasing a used motorcycle, you will also hold down your overall investment in the sport while you see if it is right for you over a long period of time.

A new motorcycle will cost more up front, or a lot more (up to $40,000 or so if you try hard), but may be cheaper to operate and easier to finance. You also have some assurance that it will not need work right away. Your choice will be dictated by a compromise between your brain, your heart, and your bank account. To assist yourself, you need to do some "work." Surf the net for several months, buy every motorcycle mag you can find, and drop by large dealers on your days off to hang out. Ask questions of every motorcyclist you know or can persuade to talk to you. This is one purchase where ignorance could cost you a lot more than money.

Insurance:

The cost of insurance will vary all over the wallet depending on where you live, the age of both you and the bike, and your "lifestyle" (i.e., how many speeding tickets have you racked up?), but I have never heard anyone describe insurance as "cheap." There are some ways to reduce your insurance cost, which will be covered in a later chapter.

Helmet:

Do not scrimp! This is an area to make sure you are getting a top-quality product, unless you have a spare head you can transplant if needed.

Accessories:

Everything from mild to wild is available for both you and your motorcycle. Essentially, you need to clothe your body in items that look good and can pass through tremendous extremes of weather at 60 mph or more. More on this later!

Other:

Any used motorcycle you buy will probably need $200 to $500 spent on it for the little things the owner "forgot" to tell you about. A new rear tire will cost about $160 on the bike...same for the front. New brake pads? A tune-up?

If you purchase a new bike you should have very few initial mechanical costs, but very soon the lust to personalize your steed may send sweaty fingers sidling toward your wallet. You will also need to purchase all of the accessories, some of which might be included when buying used.

To sum up, motorcycling can be a wonderful sport that may change your life for the better in many wonderful ways, but motorcycles are always dangerous and never inexpensive. If you can handle that, we'll move on to the specifics!

CHAPTER TWO
Accessories

When you choose to buy a motorcycle, you also choose to purchase a panoply of "support system" products that will allow you to ride safely and comfortably. Part of the joy of motorcycling is that you are not enclosed in a "cage," as in a car. In fact, hard-core biker types often refer to cars as "cages" for this reason. However, because you're not surrounded by the body of the car, you will need to purchase many items that will effectively clothe your own body with substitutes for the fenders and windshield of a car. These items can include:

- helmet (s) and visor (s)
- jacket (s)
- gloves
- pants
- boots

In addition, you may want to purchase security items, such as:

- cover
- lock
- burglar alarm

And, you most certainly will want to buy insurance. In many states it is now a legal requirement.

People who claim to be buying a motorcycle as inexpensive transportation are usually deluding themselves, or perhaps the parents who are to be the funding source. In truth, motorcycles of a medium or larger size are usually MORE expensive to purchase and operate than a small used economy car. However, if you need an excuse and this one will work for you, fine... just don't believe yourself!

CHAPTER THREE

How to Buy Helmets

Question #1: What type of helmet should I buy?

Almost all helmets are either "open face" or "full face." Open face helmets are, as you surely can imagine, open. There is nothing covering your face, which is the "open" part, while your scalp and the sides of your head are protected. Open face helmets, when combined with glasses or goggles as eye protection, get you right out there in the breeze. They offer increased vision and put you much more in touch, literally, with the motorcycle experience. Of course, their utility is easily compromised by common factors such as cold and rain.

An open face helmet can also be a style statement. It looks "cooler" to some. Obviously, an open face helmet is going to offer less crash resistance, since 40% or so of your head is open to whatever you are colliding with! They are, however, INFINITELY better than no helmet at all. If you plan to ride a motorcycle and not wear a helmet, you should immediately give this CD to someone whose intellectual capacity and reading skill will allow them to make use of it.

A full-face helmet encloses the head completely, with a face "port" of varying size covered by a clear or tinted visor that can be swung open. They are, in almost all instances, the best designs in terms of crash resistance. Since all motorcycle road racing organizations require a full-face helmet, they also look more "racy," which can be a style consideration. They offer more warmth on chilly days, and are much better at dealing with rain, not to mention large juicy bugs that choose to commit suicide by colliding with your head at a high speed.

Question #2: What does a crash helmet do?

Ah, here is an essential question. What exactly happens in a crisis situation (crash), and how can a helmet help?

Oddly enough, this was not studied until fairly recently. Much of what we know about motorcycle accidents comes from research done by Dr. Harry Hurt (is that not the most wonderful name?) at USC, beginning in the late 1960s. Dr. Hurt and a bevy of grad students studied a great many motorcycle accidents in the L.A. area by flocking to the scene and photographing, measuring, and interviewing. The results of their research were dramatic and surprising in some of the conclusions that could be drawn... First of all, in the case of fatality incidents, the percentages of the riders who were a.) drunk or b.) on a stolen motorcycle or c.) killed the first six months of riding... totaled over 100%! Statistical analysis hint: many of the deceased qualified for more than one category, and some went for the trifecta and covered all three! Avoiding alcohol and drugs, not stealing a bike, and riding safely for six months will significantly improve your health when it comes to motorcycles! That should not be too difficult a task to accomplish.

Back to the helmet itself. A helmet will not protect you from a head-on collision with a brick wall at 75 mph, nor is it designed to. Such impacts are rare. Just think about it for a moment. If you have a crash, you will be falling from a height of four feet or so onto a paved surface at some sort of speed. Your head will be bouncing off the hood or fender of a car, or off the road, and possibly both. In fact, your head will need to survive several impacts, but it is unlikely you will simply hit something very hard, head on, and stop.

Fatal motorcycle head injuries usually involve a problem with human head design. Your head was not designed for 60 mph impacts. It was designed to protect your brain from low-speed impacts (watch out for that tree) or from contacts with blunt objects (club) or sharp objects (spear). For these reasons, your brain is surrounded by hard bone, and your eyes are protected by an atoll of bone in a ring around the eyeball. This is a fine design for cave-dwelling, sheep- herding, or small town life of the Middle Ages, but design flaws begin to show with modern motorcycles capable of sustained speeds above 50 mph. Simply put, you can be killed from the inside! In a high-speed accident, your brain tends to slam into the bony shell and then bounce back across the skull and collide with the other side. Many folks have died of severe brain trauma, even though the head did not appear to be injured. Most of these people were called "helmet-less riders."

Given that, what all modern crash helmets attempt to do is to lengthen, by milliseconds, the time duration of the crash impact. They do this by a process of controlled self-destruction. When the helmet collides with a solid object, usually at a glancing angle, the inner layers of fiberglass, carbon fiber, Kevlar, and whatever other materials have been used begin to collapse, or degrade, at a controlled rate. What this does is allow your head to decelerate less abruptly, and your brain to merely slosh around in your head instead of slamming into the bony shell. The helmet is designed to absorb several such impacts and leave you shaken, but very much alive. All modern cars use the same technological concept by having crush zones built into the front and (usually) rear end designs... the car destroys itself while the occupants, in a heavily braced safety cage in the middle, walk away to deal with the insurance claims and the need to buy a new car. In the case of a helmet, you MUST replace your helmet if it has been through an accident. It may only have a scratch or two in the paint, but it has suffered severe internal damage in a valiant and evidently successful attempt to save you. It needs to be moved to a shelf as an honored memento, as well as a solid reminder to never again do what got you into the mess. It should never be worn again.

Question #3: What do I look for when buying a helmet?

Most helmet purchases, whether open or full-faced designs, are made on the basis of three variables: safety, cost, and appearance. The ordering of those three parameters will vary according to the individual, so I will attack them in alphabetical order.

APPEARANCE

Motorcyclists are an independent group of people who have their own opinions and have deliberately chosen a sport that involves a degree of risk. As such, they reserve the right to make design and color choices that fly in the face of logic and reason. This is why black is the best selling helmet color. Because it is the least conspicuous, black is, logically, the worst color, but millions of motorcyclists a year buy black helmets because they like the look. I believe it was Dr. Hurt who coined the term "conspicuity" as an important safety consideration. His studies indicated that a motorcyclist wearing a neon orange safety vest and a bright yellow or orange helmet enjoyed an enhanced margin of safety, but perhaps this is merely because you look so weird car drivers shy away from you... hey, if it works...

Helmets can also be had with various graphic designs, which may add to conspicuity. If you are buying new from a dealer and you are smart enough to work a helmet into the price negotiations, you can probably find a design with a paint scheme that matches the motorcycle, which is a cool idea. In a full-face helmet, be sure to figure in the cost of two face shields, a clear and a smoke or dark green shade for sunny days. There are also various iterations such as "chrome" and "iridium" tints for some models, which increase the space-alien nature of the helmet and may thus enhance conspicuity... or not. Some motorcyclists feel that a black helmet with a dark shield looks the most menacing and therefore enhances safety by intimidating car drivers, which is certainly possible, but only if they see you in the first place.

Best advice on appearance is to read the magazines and surf the internet looking at helmet designs until you find a "look" that suits your taste, and then base your purchase decision on cost and safety issues.

EXPENSE

When I was first lusting after motorcycles, at the age of 15, Bell Helmets had what I thought was a marvelous ad line: "If you have a $10 head, buy a $10 helmet." The price reference may provide a clue to how long ago that was, but the logic of it still holds. With some important caveats, the quality of a helmet, and to some extent the safety provided, will be reflected by the price.

I should point out that Dr. Hurt's research showed little difference in the crash results when price of the helmet was used as a variable. There was a vast chasm of a gap between helmet and no helmet, but the differences related to open and full types and by price range were much smaller.

There is little to be gained by shopping for the least expensive helmet. Instead, you should, once again, figure out what type of helmet and what appearance you desire, and work toward a price range you are comfortable with. Your desired level of safety and intended use will also enter into this complex equation.

SAFETY

A more expensive helmet can be safer, depending on why it is more expensive. I once had a Bell Star helmet, which was a very good helmet design in 1982. It had 5 layers of fiberglass. The Shoei helmet I replaced it with had 7 layers, and offered enhanced crash impact absorption qualities. My current Arai features improved materials, features, and safety, and is the best helmet I have ever owned. At a cost greater than what I paid for many entire motorcycles years ago, it could be argued that it should be! To go back to the Bell Helmets ad – I evidently now own a $700 head.

Still, you do need to find out why a more expensive helmet carries the heavy price tag. Some are replicas of paint and graphic designs worn by world famous riders. You may want to pay up to several hundred dollars more for these, but graphics and paint will not make the helmet any safer.

Weight is also a factor in helmet design. Your spinal cord was not really designed to carry large amounts of weight at the end. Designers could conceivably produce a helmet with incredible resistance to impact, but at a weight that would snap your neck, leaving you very good looking, and very dead. Compromise is always a dirty word for a designer as he or she tries to build in as much crash resistance as possible at a price that will be acceptable and a weight that will not be counter-productive.

All other factors being equal, a lighter helmet may cost more. To achieve the highest crash resistance and hold weight down, more and more exotic (rare) materials are used, and the price goes up. This is true at the pricey end of the spectrum. In less expensive helmets, lighter weight usually means less material, and they may not offer as much protection. As the consumer, you may actually want to prioritize lighter weight over crash resistance. I chose this route when purchasing a helmet for my children when they were old enough to ride on the back. I purchased a relatively inexpensive full-face helmet that was not the best in crash resistance, but offered very light weight for their still-maturing spines. They would not be riding often, or far, and I did not want the expense of a truly great helmet they would soon outgrow. Life is full of tough decisions, and this is one of them.

How the helmet fits is an important safety factor. Most helmet manufacturers use a number of different molds to create small, medium, and large helmets. Some are considered to be "round" and some "oval," referring to the overall shape of the mold (and the customer's head) when viewed from above. Their molds may or may not line up with your particular head shape! You will have a hard time changing the shape of your head, but it is pretty easy to try out different helmet brands to see which, in general, line up well with your noggin's shape. This is a strong argument in favor of buying a helmet in an actual store when you can examine it closely and try it on your own head, not a theoretical head or one measured at one circumferential point with a tape.

What you are looking for is snug but not too tight around the top of the head, with an even feeling to the fit. In a full face, the eye port must be large enough to allow you to see to the sides. A salesperson experienced in helmet fit can be a great asset here. Most helmets are secured to your head by a chin strap and a pair of "D" rings; two rings in the shape of a letter... no points for guessing which one. The chinstrap goes through both rings and back through one of them for a secure fit, and on some models any extra length can be secured to a snap so it does not flap in the wind.

In most areas of the world helmets will be required to display some sort of a safety sticker inside. There are differences in the stickers, and in what the stickers mean. Here is a short guide to the stickers used in America.

- No sticker ...this means "Do not buy this helmet."

- DOT sticker ...this Department of Transportation sticker means that the helmet complies with United States government standards, which are the product of government safety experts, political wrangling, well-intentioned and other input from elected representatives who may or may not ever have actually ridden a motorcycle, and lobbyists for both the helmet and insurance industries. Thus, a DOT sticker represents a series of holy and unholy alliances and compromises, and, despite all of that, is probably a fine helmet for you to use.

- Snell sticker... now you are getting serious. The Snell Foundation was formed in the memory of one Peter Snell, and was the first group to do any scientific testing of helmets. Peter Snell was killed in 1957 in a fairly low impact sports car racing crash when his helmet split in half. There were no standards in place at that time, and what you thought you saw in a helmet was not necessarily what you got. Since that time, Snell standards have become increasingly rigorous. The date on a Snell sticker identifies the year for the standards the helmet meets, not the year of manufacture. Thus, a Snell 2000 might have been made in 2002. In recent years Snell has moved into partitioning helmets by type, so a motorcycle helmet might meet different standards than one made for a race car. Motorcycle helmets are rarely called upon for fire protection, for instance, while race car helmets do not need as much abrasion resistance. An additional consideration for your helmet might be other uses. Many sports-car and sport bike clubs now rent local race tracks for driving education days (defined as "wheeee!") and they usually require a fairly recent Snell certification helmet for participation. Snell certifications are usually changed every 5 to 7 years, so check with the organization you will be riding or racing with, if this is a concern, and buy accordingly.

And what about a passenger? Do you ever intend to take a friend along for a ride? Is he or she any less deserving of care than you? You may have just doubled your budget!

CHAPTER FOUR
How to Buy Gloves

Gloves are normally sold in pairs, (imagine!) and in the case of motorcycle use you may need pairs of pairs. This is because your hands are exposed not only to the elements, but to several different other types of risk, and over a broad temperature range.

NOT WEARING GLOVES

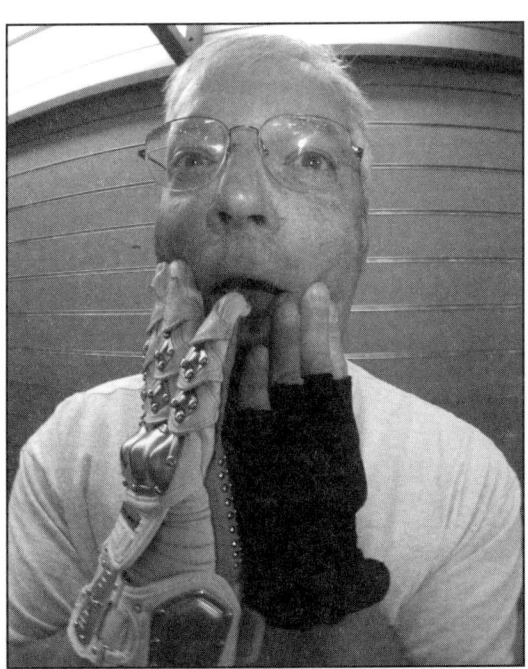

This comes under the same general heading as "Not Wearing a Helmet." I see people doing it, so I know it can be done, but I cannot fathom why anyone chooses to do it. Contemplate reality...you are sailing down a paved road at any legal speed. Look at your hands. Imagine the road surface. Now attempt, in your mind, the performance of a handstand on that road surface at the speed you are maintaining, using your bare hands.

Ouch! More likely... ouch, bounce, ouch, bounce, ouch, snap, snap ouch, ouch, groooooaaannn.

TYPES OF GLOVES

Gloves used in riding a motorcycle have to respond to many demands. They protect your hands from heat and cold and water. They resist impacts and abrasions, both during normal operation and in the unfortunate circumstances of a crash. At the same time, they need to be extremely supple to allow you to operate the controls, sometimes while performing multiple tasks. The rider of a sport bike rushing at 80 mph toward a 25 mph corner will need to operate the clutch lever several times, in concert with the left foot on the shift lever, while the right hand applies the brakes and blips the throttle at the same time, all in a coordinated rhythm with the left hand and foot. Additionally, both hands must provide a secure brace on the handlebars against the braking forces shoving the torso forward. Done correctly, it is an exhilarating ballet of coordination; done badly it can lead to disaster. Gloves that are too bulky will not allow all of this to take place, and gloves that are too thin will shred themselves to uselessness at the first hint of an impact with the road.

IMPACT RESISTANCE

Even though you may never suffer a crash, your gloves have to be designed with that expectation. The normal human response to any crash, even a clumsy incident with a footstool while walking across the living room, is to put the hands in front. On a motorcycle this often means a sliding and jarring impact against an abrasive surface of tar or concrete. To deal with this, gloves can be made with multiple layers of leather, or with steel studs embedded in the palm that are meant to slide or, in many modern designs, inserts of Kevlar and/or carbon fiber. All of these present design problems. Multiple layers of leather are only as strong as the stitching holding them together. Steel studs may work, but may also build up so much heat they burn the hands they are trying to protect. Carbon fiber, Kevlar, and other techno-wondrous materials are very expensive, more expensive than they need to be because they are "in." Gloves, like everything on a motorcycle, make a style statement. Style will always change, and in fact has to, in order to be style. The only constant is that style is always expensive. Your choice of gloves, therefore, may come down to a compromise of features and materials you want vs. cost.

WHAT NOT TO BUY

Most gloves sold in clothing or sporting goods stores will just not do. Those snazzy baseball batting gloves look the business, but are as sturdy as wet tissue paper in an accident. The trendy executive driving gloves are also too thin, and the stitching is not meant to stand up to the forces in play in a motorcycle accident. You need gloves…motorcycle gloves.

MOTORCYCLE GLOVES

Any motorcycle dealer will present an alluring array of gloves for your delectation. You get to choose your size, your style, and your preferred price range.

Road racing style gloves are thin but sturdy, and will usually incorporate steel studs or Kevlar or carbon fiber, sometimes in combinations. They will be tight fitting, and usually have a flared cuff to go over the sleeve of the leather jacket you bought, and a Velcro closure at the wrist. They are usually made in a riot of colors, and will look expensive. They are. They work well, but may not be practical on a cold day. They are also so enticing they may have a tendency to walk away if not watched carefully at all times.

Touring gloves are usually heavier, and usually black. They may have rain mitts that fold into a pouch on the back. Some have a short length of rubber down the side of the forefinger, which works very effectively to squeegee water off the visor of a full-face helmet. They will also have a gauntlet up over the sleeve, which will usually be usefully longer than what is found on the racing applications. The gauntlet may be closed with a Velcro closure, or even a zipper to snug it down.

Some affected cruiser riders go for black "shorty" gloves liberally sprinkled with holes for that "cool guy" look. They don't look as cool after you have shredded and fractured your fingers. Unless you are wearing heavy winter gauntlets on a very hot day, cooling will not be a problem, as the wind chill at any appreciable speed will provide all of the cooling you need, and usually more than you want! BMWs and other models of various brands have heated grips for this reason, and most people who have them rave at length about the rapture of warm hands, but I have no experience of them to offer.

OTHER GLOVES

I usually carry three pairs of gloves on a trip and two on an afternoon jaunt. I have two pair of heavier winter gloves. If I spend a day in the rain on a long trip, rather than fuss with waterproof covers, I just allow the gauntlets to do their best, guarded by applications of waterproofing mink oil. If they become sodden by the end of the day, I simply check into a motel instead of camping, and try to let them dry overnight. If all else fails, I can alternate them each day, if I have by mischance located myself in the middle of a vast storm system going my way.

Here's a historical note. When I first began riding motorcycles, shortly after the last dinosaur smoked that final cigarette on his way to oblivion, I prided myself on buying white leather gloves. Why? They showed up better at night. Why was this a good idea? Because in those days, dear children, your hands also functioned as the turn signals!

So then, three or four pair of gloves and away you go! The passenger? She or he can wear one of the pair you are not using.

CHAPTER FIVE
How to Buy Jackets and Rain Gear

JACKETS

Here again the plural may be the case, as any one jacket may not be able to meet all of your needs for 12 months of the year depending, of course, on where you happen to live. Once again, it's possible to ride a motorcycle without wearing a jacket, but it's a very bad idea. I once watched a young man crash his beater-bike while wearing only sandals and swimming trunks. As the medics gathered around to talk to him, his back gradually changed hues, going from white to scrubbed pink to lurid and, ultimately, running blood red. After I had deposited my lunch behind a handy bush I walked away, that day's lesson learned well.

Jackets that are used for motorcycle use come in a variety of styles and are made from a bewildering array of materials, but they all strive to meet similar design goals. They must offer comfort in an environment covering an ambient temperature range of 60 degrees or more, and at speeds from 0 to "No officer, I actually had no idea I was going that fast." They need to be at least somewhat rain-proof, or at least rain-resistant, be comfortable to wear, and be of great utility in a crash. Oh yes; if at all possible, a jacket should look "cool" as well.

WHY LEATHER?

It may seem odd that, in an age of exploding technological progress, the skins of dead cow, deer, and goats still sell very well, but leather jackets are close to ideally suited for motorcycle use. This is because the needs of the previous owner (the animal) were similar to your needs. In the same fashion as a helmet, but using much more basic design, a leather jacket is designed to save you in a crash situation by destroying itself.

Pause for thought: it may seem, in reading this book, that motorcycle crashes are a weekly experience. If they are, you have most definitely chosen the wrong sport! My last crash was in 1969, well over 100,000 motorcycling miles ago, but in purchasing all of this "stuff" as accessories it's a terrific idea to consider the worst possible scenario. By doing so, you will probably survive that worst possible scenario... and if it never comes, at least you were prepared. The Boy Scouts do have a good idea or two, y'know.

Back to the crash...so here you are, sliding down an asphalt surface at 60 mph or so. Your leather jacket will cover most of the parts of your body in contact with the road surface, and the leather will be abraded away at a rate such that you will run out of velocity and leather at about the same time. When finished, you will be allowed to utter a few oaths, as you have just written off a jacket, a helmet, gloves, and a motorcycle, but you will notice at some point that you are most definitely alive.

When purchasing a leather jacket, there are some design features to look for. Once again, just any leather jacket will not do. Men's clothing stores sell lots of leather jackets, and some of them are designed to look like motorcycle jackets, (we are SO stylin'!), but they are... most definitely... not. What you need is:

- Thick leather. Many of the fashion-statement jackets look very nice because they are made of very thin leather that will gradually "mold" itself to the wearer. A real motorcycle jacket will be of much heavier leather, and may almost seem crude by comparison. It will eventually mold itself to you, but it will take longer.

- Zippers. Buttons are useless in a crash, so you need a stout metal zipper to keep the jacket around you. Most motorcycle jackets will also feature zippers on the sleeves for a snug wrist closure, and this is handy because most motorcycle gloves have a gauntlet wrist covering to slide over the jacket sleeve the designers presume you own.

- Closures. Some casual leather jackets feature elastic fabric at the wrists and at the collar. Such fabric does a wonderful job of wicking up any rain water and storing it for you, so it can gradually seep down your chest and back and bring on hypothermia. You want a snug collar fit (quite often called a "Mandarin" collar) that will keep out wind and rain.

- Pockets. Once you are in a motorcycle jacket, you are really "in," and reaching onto an inner pocket may not be handy. Outer packets need to be accessible and to be open and closed by zippers. You do not want flaps that in the wind, will... flap.

- Armor. In recent years manufacturers have begun to insert pieces of body armor into some jackets. These will be some sort of high-tech plastic pieces that cover the upper shoulders, spine, and elbows. In some cases they are removable. They will greatly increase the protection offered in a crash, especially for the spinal cord, but with increased costs as well.

- Fit. A motorcycle jacket will usually be cut a little longer in the lower back, to cover down to your waist when leaning forward, as you do on many motorcycles. The arms may also be slightly "rotated," compared to a normal jacket, to better fit you in the posture you will assume when riding. The fit should be large enough to allow you to choose to wear a sweater or vest underneath, but not so huge that you create gaps for wind and water. One advantage to buying a jacket at a motorcycle dealer is that the salesperson helping you undoubtedly rides a motorcycle and can offer good advice. Of course, you may pay a little more for this service.

In recent years women have begun to enjoy motorcycling in increasing numbers, both as passengers and, ever more frequently, as riders. They now are numerous enough (hurray!) that manufacturers can design products with them in mind. For example, one of Harley-Davidson's most rapidly increasing demographic sales groups is women over 40. Harleys tend to have lower seat heights, for one thing, which is handy for (in general) shorter legs. In jacket design, women have a different body shape, which I have been noticing, pretty much constantly, since I was about 6 years old. A little judicious shopping in a well-stocked store can rustle up jackets that fit women, and this is a fairly recent development. Note the non- sexist use of both "well-stocked" and "development" in that sentence!

ONE-PIECE SUITS

One-piece suits are seen on all of the road racers, because they are required, among other reasons. Magazine staffers usually appear in them as well. They offer tremendous looks, and can be had in a mind-boggling array of designs, some of them quite lurid. The disadvantages are considerable, however. They are harder to put on and take off, and while strolling around on a hot day your only option is to strip the top half down and tie the sleeves around your waist. They are usually a taut fit for aerodynamics, and may not have room for a sweater or vest. They also may have few or no pockets. They are ideal for fast road riding on a warmer day, but they are also very expensive. For me, they also have the disadvantage of giving you the appearance of having something to prove. I know how fast I am, or not, and I do not feel the need to advertise. To be fair, I am tempted by the opportunity to have a set that matches both my physique and the color scheme of my bike...they do look the business for sure!

LEATHER CARE

In its previous life (literally) the leather in your jacket was constantly being renewed by the living creature wearing it. In recycled form, you will be called upon to apply from the outside some emollients that the animal applied from the inside. Mink oil, which is derived from mink that no longer need it, can be rubbed into the surface of the leather at periodic intervals. They will keep the leather supple and also impart an amazing degree of waterproofing. I have a one-piece rain suit for longer trips, but it stays at home for daily rides, as I have found that my current leather jacket will remain warm and dry for the distance home. In addition, saddle soap can be used to clean the detritus that your jacket will accumulate, including road tar, possible oil grime from the front fork seals that need to be replaced, and an amazing collection of the internal organs of a great many bugs. The application of a saddle soap and elbow grease, followed by a good massage with mink oil, will keep your jacket happy. It will also provide you with a good afternoon's break from more mundane chores such as mowing the lawn or vacuuming.

OTHER MATERIALS

Technological progress may be catching up to leather. Many companies now offer jackets and complete suits in Cordura and other fabrics that equal or exceed the properties of leather. They have not caught up in the area of looking "cool," but fashions may change at a moments notice. They are worth your consideration, especially if you apply the same fitting standards above. Many of them are now washable, as well.

OTHER TYPES OF JACKETS

Momentary observation on the roads will allow you to notice many other types and styles of jackets being worn. The good news is that any jacket is a much better idea than no jacket. Many touring riders favor satin jackets that can be had in a rainbow of colors with all sorts of adornments. Many cruiser riders prefer the classic denim. Some folks swear by snowmobile suits which, although bulky enough to make you look like an ad for Michelin tires, provide a lot of warmth and rain protection all in one. In my financially-deprived college years I wore a ski parka, which worked pretty well but would have been less than wonderful in a crash. Still, anything is much, much better than nothing.

RAIN GEAR

Here is one product whose design intent is embedded in the name. Does it keep you dry? As in all other areas, there is more to the matter than might at first meet the mind's-eye.

First of all, the rain gear is normally going to be worn over whatever other clothing you have chosen. Thus, it must be big enough to get into, while already wearing a fairly heavy jacket, pants, and boots of some kind. The attributes of fit are even more critical here, as rain has a magical ability to search your gear to find any possible point of egress. Once in, it rapidly finds a route to your back, and eventually to your crotch. Unless you are so kinky I do not want to ever meet and converse with you,

you will not enjoy the experience of ice cold water pooling in your crotch.

Most rain gear comes in a choice of three designs: jacket, jacket and pants, and one piece suit. Which one you select will be determined by your intended use, your motorcycle, and your budget.

A one-piece rain suit is ideal for a long ride in a really miserable weather. It may take a bit longer to adorn yourself, but once inside you are set for the day. I actually enjoy riding in the rain, IF it is going to be a long ride. It is peaceful and exciting at the same time, and as long as I have had time to don my chosen gear beforehand, all is well. The worst situation is a day with intermittent rain showers that occur quickly (Georgia in summer comes to mind) where you can never decide exactly what to do. Rain suits do tend to be a bit bulky, requiring the most storage space on the motorcycle, which is probably why they seem to be favored by touring motorcyclists with large saddlebags and top trunks.

A rain jacket that can be donned quickly can be very handy, and some have a handy pouch on the lower back into which the entire jacket can be folded for easy storage. If you ride short distances, and your motorcycle has excellent fenders and/or a full fairing to keep your legs dry for a while, this may be all that you need.

Rain pants are also an item that, one would assume, you put over pants you are already wearing! They will also need to fit over your boots, so most of them have some sort of snap closure to tighten up a wide lower leg. They can usually be rolled up and stored in the side pocket of a tank bag.

One useful tidbit that is never mentioned at the point of purchase is that many rain suits lose their utility when stored for long periods. I used to have a pretty good quality set of pants and jacket that spent 15 years rolled into the pockets of my tank bag. That was during the years of child-raising, so I rarely had the chance or desire to ride in the rain. When I finally needed them, they were useless! I now go with a simple pair of inexpensive rain pants for short trips than can be pulled on easily and work well. When they fail, it will be no big financial trauma to replace them.

Rain suits and jackets designed for motorcycles often come with reflective stripes for increased visibility, especially at night. My suit is marketed by Triumph, and has not only the reflective stripes but an alluring, or is that alarming, yellow color. It is certainly visible, in any case, and with my yellow helmet I resemble the outcome of a banana and a grade D science fiction movie about nuclear power. This suit takes several minutes to put on – but it works very well for that all day romp in the rain.

Rain boots need to be easy to put on, and since they are last donned this can be a considerable consideration. You should shop for them while wearing everything else you will have on at the time. There are, as in everything else in this chapter, a plethora of available products that will do the job. For really severe riding in Seattle winter rain weather, I have a pair of boots made for use on snowmobiles – water proof and very warm. Also very ugly, but on the days I am using them, they match the weather.

Try to purchase your rain gear after everything else is in hand, so you can shop while wearing all of your stuff and with the knowledge of what storage space you have and what kind of riding you will be doing.

Once again, the passenger's needs may need to be considered, although relatively few inexperienced motorcyclists venture out on a rainy day with a passenger. It's difficult to find a person who wants to go, for one thing!

CHAPTER SIX
How to Buy Pants and Boots

Well, obviously, jeans are the way to go right? If you survey the motorcycles sashaying down most any road, jeans would appear to be the riders' apparel of choice. Why would anyone wear anything else?

Jeans are not at all a bad choice. They are (relatively) inexpensive, long-wearing, and certainly stylish. They offer some degree of warmth, and some degree of abrasion resistance, although not much. Primarily they are something almost everyone already has, and thus they are a practical answer for day to day wear.

However, all is not for the best in all conditions. Jeans, being made of cotton, not only do not repel water, but actually absorb water very effectively. Water will "wick" up cotton pants until it gets somewhere you would much prefer to keep dry. They can become very cold in a very great hurry. They also do not last long, as measured in feet, in the event of a crash. They'll shred quickly, and the next thing to shred will be you. By shopping in the back pages of motorcycle magazines, you can find jeans with hidden internal armor that address this last concern.

If you plan to ride to work, and if you need to look "professional' at your job, you will need to carry your dress slacks separately or invest in some sort of riding suit. Note: I have always thought the phrase "professional dress" to be a slam to anyone who may have chosen a career where they would not have to wear "professional" clothes...people like me. My work "uniform" is a Cycle Barn shirt and black jeans, and so I am not professional. Pooh. Anyway, do not wear suit slacks and wing-tip shoes to ride your motorcycle, please! The cuffs flap in the wind, the safety afforded both legs and feet is nil, and worst of all, you look like a total dork!

Amusing anecdote: Over twenty years ago, when Harleys first began to be ridden by upscale folk, I worked for a time on weekends in the Cycle Barn parts department. We were always amused by the bankers and attorneys that came in. You could tell them by the brand new jackets and the brand new helmets, but primarily by their jeans... they had pressed creases in them!

There are other types of pants available, of course, and some of them might be useful to you. Some of them, on the other hand, (or leg) should be avoided!

LEATHER PANTS

Leather pants are a good idea, once you get past the cost, which can be quite high. You will, however, need to shop very carefully. Due to the sitting posture, which can be quite contorted on a sport bike, you will need enough room in the legs and rear to be comfortable, especially in the knees. Just as when shopping for a jacket, you want to look for a fairly heavy weight of leather, and for zipper closures on pockets. I would also recommend shopping for them with the boots you intend to wear, as some combinations of pants and boots require the pants to be on the inside and some on the outside, and often it is only one or the other. The pants outside will be a little more relaxed in fit, while the pants inside the boots will not have flapping leg ends and may (or may not) make you feel "racy." The pant legs inside may also allow rain water to run right down the inside of the boots, but they will also be warmer. The choice(s) are yours.

Although the initial cost will be high, the investment in leather pants will be paid back immediately, should you ever suffer an accident. Leather pants also provide a much broader comfort range in terms of temperature. As long as the bike is moving, you will normally not be uncomfortably hot in the sun, although walking around in the desert is not a good idea. Leather is much warmer than the denim in jeans, and if you buy them just a bit large, you will be able to wear long johns underneath and be comfortable down to the point of "why am I out here today?" temperatures. Although available in many colors, motorcyclists who choose leather seem to prefer black. This is due to both tradition and practicality, as black leather is relatively easy to keep clean. Colored leather is dyed (unless you can find a purple, blue, or red cow), and the dye may wear in unusual patterns where you and the seat make contact.

One item to keep in mind with leathers is that you will need to maintain your body weight and shape over a period of time to use them. They are much more expensive to replace, so an extra helping of lasagna here and there can be very expensive! This limitation can work for you or against you, depending on your point of view.

You can also buy "chaps," usually in black leather. These are made to be worn over jeans, and have zippers down the sides and an open crotch area for ease of donning. They offer some advantages, at the expense of needing storage space for them if you intend to take them off during the day. One of the advantages is that almost anyone, particularly women, looks fabulous in them! One of the disadvantages is that they are of little utility in the event of a good solid downpour, as my daughter proved on a New Year's Day ride last year.

HIGH TECH

There are, every day, new fabrics coming on the market which attempt to meet or exceed the capabilities of leather while retaining most of the advantages of jeans. They can often be made to be washable, and come in a variety of colors and styles. Once again you will want to shop for quality of stitching and fit and finish, and look for the advantageous use of pockets with secure closures. Every year these products get a little closer to meeting or exceeding the performance of leather, but old dunderhead traditional fogies like me will probably stick to dead cows for the foreseeable future. You, however, might prefer the more modern gear.

PLASTICS

Just say no. Whether referred to as "parachute pants" or by some other trendy name, do not buy pants made of synthetic materials based on plastic, especially in a baggy style. The bagginess will get old very quickly in the wind, and should you ever fall off, things will get very much worse in a big hurry. Synthetics, when heated and abraded, both shred and melt, and have the distressing tendency to melt inside the abrasions you are giving yourself. The emergency room personnel will not think highly of you. Actually, in my experience, emergency room personnel do not think highly of motorcyclists anyway.

In conclusion, you can invest a great deal of time in the selection of pants, or none at all, if I can assume you already own some jeans. Pants can be put pretty much at the end of your shopping list, but you might want to plan your accessory purchases with a mind to where you want to end up. If you want to purchase leather pants eventually, buy a jacket that will work with leather pants, both from a functional and style point of view. In this one area, at least, your passenger can probably take care of his or her own needs!

CHAPTER SEVEN
How to Buy Footwear

Boots are another clothing area that seems simple, but is not. After all, almost everyone has some sort of hiking boots and these will do, sort of...

TENNIS SHOES

No. Tennis shoes are readily available in your closet, but bring with them a plethora of disadvantages. They are not very resistant to either wind or water, and so are soon likely to be uncomfortable. Any objects thrown up by the car ahead, or your own front tire, will meet little protective resistance from a tennis shoe. Expensive tennis shoes will quickly become limp and useless balls of filth when exposed to the grime and dust of a couple of days of riding.

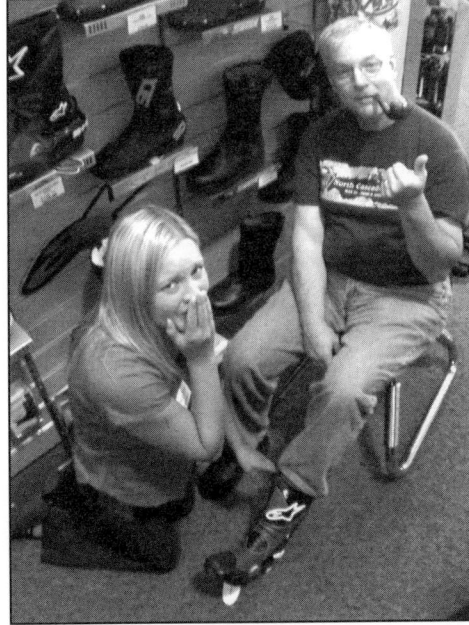

Let's look, again, at the design requirements for motorcycle footwear in the worst of cases. In an impact, you want to have as much of your lower leg as possible encased in protection of some sort. If possible, it is best to let your footwear take all of the abuse.

If you are planning on wearing loafers, or sandals, or no shoes at all, please sell your motorcycle immediately. OK, I have to confess: I did wear loafers while riding my motorcycle... once. That was the day I crashed. In any case, please give yourself and your feet at least a chance, as I did not. (My feet were not injured in my crash, but that was due to dumb luck. Besides, I had enough other worries with the broken shoulder... that was also the only day I rode without a jacket.) Let he who is without sin cast the first motorcycle.

Please don't shop for boots just after you've run a 25k marathon – okay!?

BOOTS

Hiking boots, because they encase the foot in a thicker shell that has been designed to offer at least some abrasion protection, are a big step up from tennies. Sorry about the pun. However, the recent trend toward "sport" hiking boots that are cut below the ankle does the motorcyclist no favors. If possible, you would like to have a boot that covers well above the ankle. In an accident, a foot and lower leg trussed up in a solid boot will probably do very well.

If you have rugged hiking boots, especially those that rise above the ankle level, you will be fine, but you may want to consider that last step (arghh, another pun) and go to motorcycle boots.

Motorcycle boots are usually made of leather, and may or may not have protective pads of various plastics, Kevlar, carbon fiber, and the miracle material being invented as I write this. They usually rise well up the shin toward the knee, and can be designed to go over the pant leg or underneath it. It is important to decide which way you want to go before buying the pants and/or the boots. Most motorcycle boots are donned by sliding the foot in from the rear, with a sturdy zipper up the back, although there are other designs as well. I used to ride with a friend who had lovely knee high boots made for fox hunting, of all things. They had no zippers up the back at all, and I could never figure out how he got them on!

You need to be careful about exactly what the boot you are purchasing is designed to do. Some road-racing models have the leg canted forward from the ankle for greater comfort in a full racing crouch. They are not very comfortable if your bike does not require that posture, and are not meant for casual strolls around the campground. The classic "engineer" boots (railroad, not aeronautical) are a traditional style favored by many cruiser riders, but they do not offer a great deal of support, as they tend to be rather loose from the ankle up. The same can be said for cowboy boots, although their devotees will not consider anything else, so any discussion is moot. Some hunting boots offer lace-up fronts that look spectacular, but that lacing is going to have to handle possibly hours of 60 mph shotgun rain, and few such lacing systems can. Some boots are marketed as being able to fit under dress pants and do double duty as shoes for the office, but I think this is more than a bit of a stretch.

Once again, a standard clothing store will not be the place to go. Some military surplus stores may offer boots that will do, but most of us will find what we want in a motorcycle dealership. If you choose to order boots by mail, it would be a very good idea to send tracing of EACH of your feet, rather than a guess as to what size you wear. Shoe sizing systems vary around the world, for no discernible reason that I know of, but a tracing will allow a good boot maker to offer you a perfect fit, and possibly a perfect and different fit for each foot. I used this system when ordering a set of boots from Frank Thomas in England in 1980 or so. I went through a couple of soles and heels, but the boots still looked wonderful when I gave them to a dear friend. She had them resoled and slightly re-sized, and they are now entering their third decade of faithful service, offering classic looks, comfort, and safety.

You might also take a peek at the sole of the boots you are buying. My Frank Thomas boots came with steel cleats at the back of the heel, which may have been great for wear resistance, but I felt like a complete moron on camping trips while traipsing around a grocery store, sounding like the entire cast of "Tap" on a break! I was relieved when they finally wore down enough to be replaced with some nice quiet rubber heels.

My current AlpineStar boots are of the road race variety. They are not as comfy, but offer all sorts of technological and materials improvements that make them a much safer bet. Boots like this can be purchased in sedate colors, or with wild combinations of trendy flash graphics, depending on customer preference.

I also have a pair of Sidi basic touring boots that are plain black and appear to be completely waterproof. Nowhere near as dramatic as the Alpinestars but I wear them about eight times as often.

It may sound surprising, but a good pair of warm and secure boots can dramatically increase your comfort and enjoyment when riding. When your feet are warm and dry and secure, the rest of you is free to concentrate on the road ahead.

In this area, your passenger's needs are a little less dramatic. She or he is shielded from a lot of the wind and rain and road detritus by the bulk in front...that would be you... so hiking boots would be OK in most circumstances.

CHAPTER EIGHT
Buying Your Motorcycle

OK, let's spend some money! By this point, you've decided what type and size of motorcycle you wish to buy. You may have narrowed your selection down to a particular brand or model. It's time to consider whether to buy new or used, and from a dealer or a private party.

BUYING NEW FROM A DEALER

Buying your motorcycle brand new from a dealer has many advantages. In this modern era, the motorcycle is quite likely to be perfect, literally, when you take ownership. This is a claim which cannot be made with confidence for any used bike. If you live in a large metropolitan area, you probably have more than one dealer for a particular brand, handy for comparison shopping. Although the initial cost of a new bike will be higher, your subsequent costs will be lower for at least a couple of years. If you're financing the purchase, a new bike is usually much easier to deal with for you, the dealer, and the financing institution, because its value is pretty well agreed upon. For my three most recent purchases, I never visited the bank, and I had the pleasure of riding the motorcycle for a week while papers were faxed back and forth. Licensing was all taken care of for me, and the plates duly arrived in the mail.

When you enter the dealership, you're at a bit of a pricing disadvantage. The dealer knows how little he or she can accept to sell the motorcycle, but they are under no moral or legal obligation to share this information with you. You may know what the list price is, but the dealer may or may not have received incentives or rebates from the manufacturer. These can change from month to month depending on sales rates for each model. The dealer also, presumably, knows a great deal more about motorcycles than you do. In addition, the dealer knows how much it cost to put the motorcycle on the floor in terms of preparation, delivery, and so forth, and how much money, if anything, that particular motorcycle is eating each month in financing costs.

You, on the other hand, are the customer, and you have the ultimate power: you can always choose not to buy. Remember that! Here are a few steps that may help you along the way to having the key to that shining new steed placed in your eager, sweating, and trembling hand.

1. Research

The more you research, the better informed you'll be. You may spend less, but more importantly, you're much more likely to be pleased with your purchase. In 1977 I had the chance to buy a new motorcycle with a squeeze of the profits from a change of house. The spousal promise made was that another motorcycle would not be needed for ten years. That Yamaha triple was a staunch ally for 22 years, so I followed through pretty well on that one. To prepare for what was an enormous expense for a young family at that time, I researched the topic... for 6 months. I read every scrap I could find on both the brand new design of the triple and on several other models being considered. Several dealers were visited, including some who had motorcycles I was not particularly interested in, but that fell in the same general price and use bracket. I talked to every motorcyclist I knew or could meet. By the time I was ready to shop, Yamaha had been building them for nine months, which increased (at the time) the odds of buying a good one, and I knew pretty much all that there was available to know about that model and several others. I knew what the cost would be before I entered the dealer's door.

2.   Do not shop alone!

You need a friend to accompany you, one who will serve as your advocate and as a leash. Being knowledgeable about motorcycles can be a help, but is not absolutely necessary. In preparing for our ZRX purchase, my wife patiently listened to me prattle about the topic for several days. She asked a lot of questions about exactly what it was I wanted in a new bike, and even took notes. She made me prioritize my desires, so I would not be swayed by chrome and paint and make a rash decision. As we drove to the dealership she grilled me like a prosecuting attorney, taking more notes, and the process of talking through her questions helped us both focus on what I really wanted.

Your assistant should be given, at the very least, a "30 minute veto." It's very easy to buy a motorcycle quickly, and almost always a very bad idea. If your assistant has hashed out with you in advance what sort of motorcycle you want, he or she will usually be able to tell when you are in the process of talking yourself into something else. Any good salesperson knows that customers will often persuade themselves to buy what you want them to buy, if you simply listen carefully and nod your head at the self-talk. Your assistant has to be given the authority to suggest a walk or a cup of coffee, so you can explain your apparent change of thinking. A really good salesperson will not mind this, because consummating a sale with a happy customer is the only way to create a repeat customer.

3.   Look at a lot of bikes.

If you have your heart set on a specific model, try to visit two or three dealers. If you're interested in a particular performance category, such as large cruiser, look at many competing brands. Do not ignore used models of your intended purchase. They will tell you a lot about how that model holds up to a year or two of use.

Your magazine research will help you assess a myriad of statistics and performance test results, but no magazine staff rides like you do, or has your exact taste. The bottom line these days is that almost every new motorcycle produced is a worthy design, and the last place finisher in a comparison test is still an excellent machine. It probably lost in the balloting of four or five experienced riders by a very narrow and usually subjective margin. If it makes your heart sing, you probably should buy it.

4.   Be willing to negotiate.

If you can afford it, just write a check for the first number the salesperson mentions, and everybody will be happy. In the real world, for most of us, you're going to want to or need to pay less, which means you will need to negotiate. Negotiation does not have to be ugly or rancorous. It will be easier if you have some things to negotiate with. Do you want anything else with the bike? Have a list of accessories prepared in advance. Helmet? Two helmets? Tank bag? Jacket? Gloves? The more things you intend to buy, the more room to negotiate the dealer will discover. The dealership needs to make a profit on these items, but for a big ticket item like a motorcycle they are usually willing to take less or no profit on some small items to swing the deal. They're happy because they're moving more product, and you're happy because you would've been buying these items for full retail by themselves.

Do keep in mind that the amount of wriggle room the dealer is willing to create will depend on the model and the time of the year. For some models likely to sell out for the foreseeable future, the price may very well be the price. If it is a rare bike, the price may be more than list… sometimes a lot more. It is a free country, and if someone will come along very soon willing to pay more than you, why on earth should the dealer sell it? Would you? Your research should help here. If you happen to be shopping in late November for a model just superceded by a new design, you may be in for a dramatic bargain! Even on the most popular model, however, you can often create some sort of a deal on the accessories you have previously scouted out at that dealer.

5.   Be willing to leave.

Do you have to buy the motorcycle today? Would it hurt to get a price from another dealership? How many of these are there? Buyer's lust is very real, and it works very well for the salesperson.

6.   Don't be a jerk!

The salesperson is just trying to sell the motorcycle, and she or he has a right to sell it for the highest possible profit. They are not out to cheat you. If you feel that they are, you should not buy anything from them, ever. There is also something to be said for the overall "feel" of the dealership. My wife wanted to buy our ZRX from Cycle Barn (before I worked there) because she liked the people and the store. This is worth something to you, and to the dealer.

I did not go for the salesperson's first offer, which was unreasonably high, as I suspected. The dealership did not go for my first offer, which was unreasonably low, as I intended. The price we reached was fair, although I probably could have done better if I had hung in there for a couple of hours.

The benefit was that the salesman was not stressed, and threw in a can of good chain lube after the deal was done because he knew my previous bike had been a shaft drive. He also had made a profit on the deal, although about $1000 less than his first offer... so he could "afford" to be a nice guy. When I discovered the following week that one of the rear view mirrors was very slightly fogged, just enough so that a monkey standing on his head at noon during an eclipse might notice it, there was no problem at all with exchanging it for an imperceptibly clearer one. Would that have happened if I had felt the need to be a jerk to show how tough I am?

When I dropped by the next few times they were happy to see me, and of course eager to sell me more stuff. I sent a friend there to buy another bike. That is how the system is supposed to work.

If you feel uncomfortable at any point in the process, use your American freedom and leave! You are the customer, and your money will talk through your feet. When I had previously visited another dealership to look at the same model, I stood for several minutes in front of a ZRX while several trendy young male salespeople ignored me. I tried to look interested and not portray the body language that says "leave me alone." Nothing. That's fine. They clearly did not want or need my $8000 worth of business.

I once took a friend to a sports car lot in Seattle, because he had decided he wanted a sports car. I had been to this lot when shopping for a Porsche, and my family and I had been deluged with friendly folk looking to help us in any way. In this case I wanted some time, so I deliberately parked my car in a hidden place and snuck Alvin onto the lot...I wanted to be able to show him, alone, what was available. We looked at various models of Porsche and Corvette and Ferrari, and in most cases he did not know what they were, so the education was total!

Alvin does corporate law for a large bank, and has the ability to buy almost any car he likes... with his charge card if he prefers. He really liked the flared fender '67 Corvette coupe...the 427... but I persuaded him it might not be the ticket for rush hour traffic! After awhile I noticed that nobody was approaching us, even though we were by now standing in the middle of the lot.

His initial sports car education now complete, we left to go look elsewhere at privately sold used sports cars of various makes. Two hours later, (I can be slow) it hit me. My friend is black. That's why we had been ignored! As a white kid from the suburbs who grew up enthralled with Martin Luther King, I understand racism, but I don't get much chance to see it in action. I was so enraged I wanted to go back and raise a holy stink. Alvin just smiled, content that I had learned MY lesson for the day.

BUYING USED FROM A DEALER

Buying used from a dealer can be the best or the worst of times. You can buy an excellent example of a model, or a real dog, but you will probably pay more for it either way. Here are some things to be aware of in considering buying used.

In many areas, there are laws that pertain to what lawyers call "implied warranty of merchantability." What this means to real people is that what is being sold needs to be what the seller states it is. A 1999 Triumph described as being in "great condition" should not have the engine collapse a week later, for example. Because lawsuits against a business can be more economically viable than those brought against an individual, many dealers do not want to risk the potential damage involved in selling a "cheap" used motorcycle that may have a lot wrong with it - mechanical flaws and damage that even the dealership does not know about. Therefore, at most dealerships, the used motorcycles on offer will be relatively recent models.

It might pay to pause and wonder why the used bike is there in the first place. An individual can almost always make more money on a motorcycle by selling it privately than by trading it in, so why is the motorcycle with the dealer? It might be that:

- The individual used their bike as part of the negotiations on a trade-in, and was sufficiently well endowed financially to not want the extra bother of selling the motorcycle. It is spotless inside and out and has been maintained by the dealership's own service department. This is much more common than I would have believed before going to work for Cycle Barn. We usually have several bikes on the used floor with less than 5,000 miles, and one or two with only a couple of hundred miles – truly amazing. My ZX12R had been treated to an Akrapovic exhaust system, a Power Commander III, a tinted windshield, and a rear fender eliminator kit, all at considerable expense, and the bike was traded in with 572 miles on the odometer.

- The individual was financially over-extended, and could not make the payments. The motorcycle in front of you has been left outside in all weathers, and has never had the oil changed.

- The machine was seized in a police drug bust.

- The dealer purchased it from an estate sale or auction.

In some cases, dealers can get very good deals from auctions and police sales that they may hear about that you do not. A local dealer sold a perfect Ducati 916 with 400 miles on the odometer. The original owner died in an altercation with police, a fairly common occurrence in his chosen career... drug dealing.

If you find a model that you like, ask if there is any service documentation. If the dealer has documentation that makes a sale more likely, they will show it to you. If not, the salesperson will merely tell you she does not know where it is, which is probably true. This does not mean the motorcycle is a bad buy, but it does create another question to be tossed into the mix.

Look for signs of casual user and crash abuse...scratched up clutch levers and grips...careless scratches in the paint, and so forth. If the motorcycle is dirty, just walk away. If the dealer is too lazy to wash it, their folks are also too lazy to want to make you a happy customer.

Signs of more serious abuse, such as racing, are a little more hidden. Small holes in drain plugs usually indicate safety wiring for road racing. You may be able to see scratches on the handlebars or elsewhere, indicating a lot of time spent tied down in a trailer on the way to and from the races. Scratches may appear down low on the fairing, if fitted, from extreme cornering angles, and the bottoms of the foot pegs will be beveled away. There may be an aging technical inspection sticker. Perhaps you WANT an ex-race bike for instant ersatz street credibility, but you need to know you're buying a bike that has been taken to the very limits of its performance envelope, and possibly past them, repeatedly.

Of course, if you want to get involved in production road racing, you might be shopping for just such a bike in the first place. If so, read up on the rules for the racing organization you will be joining, so you know what models are accepted. You don't need to worry about which model will be the most competitive in a particular class, because it will take you a year or two to make yourself competitive, and at that time you can worry about having the "right" model.

If you find a used bike at the dealer that you want to buy, the same system applies as in the new bike section. See if you can broker a deal to include other accessories you will need to buy, negotiate in good faith, and always retain your ability to say "No" and walk away. There are lots and lots of used motorcycles.

BUYING USED FROM A PRIVATE PARTY

Obviously, many used motorcycles are purchased in private transactions. Although some of the same issues pertain as when shopping at a dealer, there are additional factors as well. I have purchased many used motorcycles and cars over the years, and learned a thing or two, sometimes the hard way. In my next life I plan to be a wealthy person and only buy new, but that is another story. Here are some techniques I have found useful in this life:

- Research. Once again, knowledge is your friend. Read up on all of the road tests published when your chosen model was new. Secret trick... often you can learn the weaknesses of a given model by the road test of the model that superceded it. Magazines thrive on new bike sales, so they have an unfortunate habit of waiting to point out design flaws until the motorcycle has been replaced. THEN they go back and trash the bike they raved about previously, letting you in on all of the "everybody knows" flaws they did not print when the model was new.

    You can also do research with your friends and relatives who ride. You need to be careful here, as some of their information may be wildly skewed in favor of their own experience and taste. Motorcycle riding is a very personal thing, and there are thousands of good folks who have always ridden only one type or brand of bike, and are just sure it would be perfect for you. They will go to great lengths to disparage any bike that does not fit their own personal pigeon-hole slot of what is good.

If you do have a friend or relative who is experienced enough to know a thing or two, yet relaxed enough to be able to assist you in buying a bike for you and not for him or her, then you have a terrific asset to talk things over with, and even to take along shopping with you. In my experience, most motorcyclists LOVE to shop for bikes, so you may have more of a problem getting your loud mouth Uncle Larry to NOT go along than you do finding a reliable expert who will be genuinely helpful, in the same manner as outlined in buying a new bike.

- Residence. I have made good purchasing decisions by looking at how and where the person lives. I bought a perfect Honda 450 from a man whose entire house and garage were dust and lint free. The bike was locked up with a chain, under a cover, inside a garage with a floor much cleaner than my kitchen. OK, I was single at the time! Without overstressing the point, I have found the manner and residence of the owner of a used machine to be the most reliable purchasing guide of all.

- Owner Test. Have the owner ride the motorcycle up and down the block. He will ride it the same way he has been riding it since he bought it. Are you impressed? Does the motorcycle sound good? Does it appear to operate well? The owner may refuse to let you take it for a ride, and this is not necessarily a bad thing. If you do not have insurance or a license endorsement to ride, why should he? If he will not let you drive it, then he has not let other idiots tromp it around the block, either. (Sorry about the "other.") Maybe he will take it for a short test drive with you on the back as a passenger. In this case, once again, you are evaluating the way the owner rides as much as the motorcycle.

After that you use pretty much the same keys you would at the dealer. However, buying it can be a little different. You may need to arrange to meet the owner at the bank that actually owns the title. Doing the exchange at a bank is a good idea anyway if a large sum of money is involved.

Hopefully, your buying experience will be a lot of fun because you did your research beforehand and went into the experience knowing what to expect. If you feel uncomfortable at any time, like when your forehead is tingling because your conscience is desperately trying to warn you about something you are too eager not to see, listen to yourself, or pay attention to your friend doing an impersonation of an alarmed Silent Bob …and stop.

CHAPTER NINE
Buying Insurance

Insurance is one of those issues in life that, while not enjoyable, is preferable to the alternatives. Place it in the same category as your two annual trips to your dentist. I like my dentist, but the two check-up visits are not the highlights of my calendar. I like my insurance agent, too, but the checks do sting a bit.

A motorcycle, with you on it, weighs between 500 and 1000 pounds. Almost any bike you buy will be able to attain 60 mph. An object of that weight traveling at that speed carries a lot of kinetic energy, and that energy will have to be dissipated by something. If the something is property or the person of someone else, a tremendous amount of damage can occur, and the legal and financial responsibility for that damage may land at your doorstep.

Besides, carrying insurance is now the law in many states, and we do wish to be law-abiding citizens.

Paying may be a cost of the enjoyment of motorcycles, but there is no reason to pay more than necessary. How much you pay will be determined by many factors, including the bike, your age, residence, income, and even sex. Is this legal? Yes.

Insurance is the only area of our modern culture where sexism, racism, ageism, and other "isms" are all legal, as long as the mainframe computers that crunch statistics can provide data that appears to support the bias. Teen-age boys pay more for insurance because the computers indicate that they are far more likely to create a loss scenario for the insurance company. One ironic trend is that teen-age girls, in the past decade or so, have been celebrating their (relative) equality by driving almost as poorly as teen boys, and so their rates are catching up. Teens with higher grade point averages rack up fewer accidents, etc. The same logic applies to bikes.

To reduce your insurance rates, focus on these ten key factors.

1. Grow Old. I know – out of your control, but I think it is amusing. Once you pass 25, for most companies – the insurance gets a lot less expensive.
2. Pass the MSF class – that is almost a guaranteed 10% savings, but check with your insurance company.
3. Buying the appropriate model. A friend who is an EMT maintains that 600cc

sport bikes with temporary paper license plates indicating their newness are the most crashed bikes by far. He should know. Your insurance company does, too. You might call an agent and ask for a list of bikes that are relatively inexpensive to insure.
4. Live in a house with a garage – rates are lower.
5. Lock up the bike in the garage.
6. Join the American Motorcycle Association – some insurance companies give a discount here, as they feel that people who are involved are a better bet. In fact, the AMA also offers insurance.
7. "Bundle" your policies. If you have a house and a car or cars, look for a company where you can insure everything with the same firm – it will probably save you a lot of money. In some cases there will be discounts for multiple cars and/or multiple bikes.
8. Avoid accidents in your car. Well duh, but a driving record is a driving record. At the risk of preaching, never driving anything under the influence of alcohol or drugs would be a nifty idea.
9. Do not speed. I am not sure of the statistical validity here. I suspect this is too tempting to be ignored by insurance companies. Everyone assumes that speeding tickets are a link to insurance losses in accidents. It's difficult to own a motorcycle and not speed – particularly a

sport bike, so you might aim for simply not speeding anywhere you are liable to get a ticket – like major routes.

10. Shop! With universal access to a computer, it takes only minutes to get a good sample of five or ten rates from different companies.

CHAPTER TEN
Your Everyday Riding System

It's just terrific to have a willing steed parked in the garage, ready to go on adventures on a moment's notice. You can ride your motorcycle to work, on a week-long trip, or just... anywhere. No matter how you plan to use your bike on a given day, however, a simple and repeatable system will make life better for the both of you.

SECURITY

Hopefully, your motorcycle is parked inside and has some sort of cover and security system you have devised. Take your time in removing the cover and lock system. Have a place where each item goes, and do the steps in the same order each time. By doing so, you slow the brain down from its "normal" frenetic multi-tasking in preparation for the

single-mindedness you will require while riding. You can also prevent embarrassing and expensive mistakes. As an example, I have a very heavy lock that goes through one of the front brake discs. I always remove that first, and place the lock in the same spot on the workbench or inside the tank bag, depending on whether or not I will need it on the ride. I make sure this is done before I ever put the key in the ignition, as this will prevent me from moving the motorcycle with the lock still attached, which could result in a broken lock, broken disc, broken fairing, or (most likely) a very red face.

Having said that, there are those who argue that the deductible on your theft insurance will be less than the damage you will do when you inevitably forget to take the disc lock off. This position gained a lot of credibility for me when I, you guessed it, forgot the remove the disc brake lock. I now lock up the bikes in the garage, but not when I am out with others and more prone to be distracted by conversations.

INSPECTION

Take a moment to look over the motorcycle with a rag or towel in your hand. You're looking for any dust or dirt you can easily remove, assuming you have consumed the chapter on keeping your motorcycle clean. A relatively spotless motorcycle is a happy motorcycle, and one that breaks down less. OK, maybe a little weak on logic and fact, but go with it anyway.

The REAL reason you're doing this is to train your mind as to what each section of your motorcycle is supposed to look and feel like when all is well. You do not need to be a mechanic, or even to have any mechanical aptitude. If you both eyeball and physically go over the motorcycle each day for 60 seconds before you ride, your mind will map out how things are supposed to look and feel. The day a tire has lost 10 pounds or pressure, or an axle cotter pin has failed and a nut loosened, you will notice the difference in appearance. You may or may not know what is wrong, but you will know SOMETHING is wrong, and you or a friend can make things right before you ride again.

Of course, as you get in the habit of doing this, you will also become more familiar with the mechanical nature of the beast, and more comfortable with your knowledge of what each part does. As a bonus, your motorcycle will always be just that little bit cleaner, and that can only be a blessing.

ACCESSORIES FOR THE DAY

Take the time to figure out what you need for where you are going. I hope you have figured out places on the bike to store a tool kit, a first aid kit, some sunglasses, and perhaps a jacket. If so, do you need a tank bag today? Saddlebags?

I take every accessory off almost every time I bring the bike home for the day. This prevents any moisture from getting trapped under a tank bag or saddlebag, and also forces me to think a little bit more before a ride. What I am trying to do is add a few minutes to the starting procedure, so my mind will have a better chance of attaining full-on motorcycle riding mode before I am out on the street.

Of course, in the old days, the motorcycles themselves took care of this. They usually needed daily maintenance to be operable, and often featured complex starting rituals that took a considerable amount of time, and that is if everything went well. This may have been a drag, but it did ensure the mental preparedness of the rider, who was usually all warmed up, mentally and physically, well before the bike. On a modern superbike, a careless rider can be moving at 140 mph about 15 seconds after deciding to go for a ride, and that is not really a good thing!

Before I leave, I want to be assured that I am carrying no more than I need to, but that I do have shades, gloves, tools, first aid kit, spare shield, and possibly a hat.

PREPARING THE RIDER

OK, the bike is ready; now for the rider. You have helped yourself a lot by taking the time to prepare the motorcycle, which was also time used to prepare yourself. Now you don whatever gear is appropriate for the day, with the helmet going on just before the gloves finish up. Most modern motorcycles have electric starters and can be ridden away almost immediately, and only waste fuel when left idling for several minutes, so I now start the bike when I am ready to go. Your needs will vary greatly depending on the bike, of course, but if it is a street bike of less than 5 years of age it probably does not need to sit and idle for several minutes.

WHEN THE HELMET DROPS...

My job at Cycle Barn is full of projects in various stages of completion, phone calls that need to be returned, meetings to prepare for, columns to write, and on and on. I have a wife. I have two adult children. I have bills. NONE of these things, and none of the mental joys and/or agonies that each can produce can be allowed to intrude on the motorcycle experience. I try very hard to use the helmet coming down over my head as a sort of shutter... all of the "stuff" of my life stops...period. With my helmet on, I am not a father, husband, writer, or a person whose credit can exceed his good sense. I am just a motorcyclist, and will be one until the helmet comes off. My mantra is a simple sentence: "When the helmet drops, the bullshit stops." If I am particularly distracted I say it out loud, or at least mouth the words. It works.

While you're riding, the other parts of your life are to be put on hold. Not to worry! Benjamin Franklin once said that 90% percent of what we worry about never happens, and he was right. Almost none of the many little traumas, worries, and fantasies running hot laps around your head at any particular time will be damaged by being put on hold for a few hours, or even several days. In fact, you may find that a good brisk ride on the motorcycle, focusing ONLY on the motorcycle, will allow you to return to your normal concerns refreshed. Answers to problems that were insoluble before may suddenly appear with great clarity. This will not work in a car, of course, because cars are too easy to drive!

THE FIRST MILE

You may have noticed road racers spending a good part of a warm-up lap swerving back and forth, at times with great violence. They also may speed up rapidly and slow down with great force. They are trying to warm up the oil, the brake pads, and the rubber in the tires, all of which are going to be called upon to deliver physics-defying performance immediately after the imminent start of the race. I do some of the same things for the first block or two.

Now, lets us just calm down here a bit. The tires and brakes on a modern motorcycle will work competently from cold in a street environment. There is no little need to warm up the tires and brakes for riding on the street. I am not. I am trying to warm up ME.

When you think about it, there is probably nothing you do in your day that is remotely like riding a motorcycle. When I meander down my local street, swerving back and forth a bit and working the throttle and brakes, I am making sure everything works, including me, before I absolutely have to be sure everything works when that semi decides to run the stop sign. You don't need to be violent about it, but a controlled swerve or two from side to side and an application of both brakes will ensure all is well. Doing this will make you want to look in the mirrors, thereby checking on their position.

OK... now let's ride!

CHAPTER ELEVEN
The Developmental Stages of a Motorcyclist

...and how to survive them!

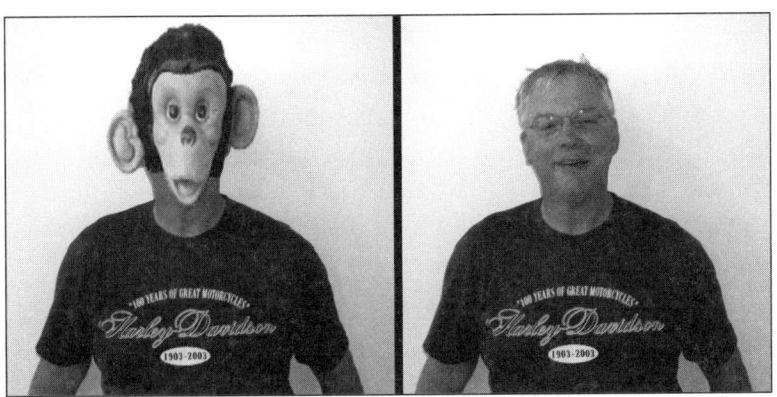

All of us change our approach to motorcycling as we gain experience. We start with that first ride on the back of a motorcycle, perhaps Dad's or one ridden by a family friend, or a teenage date. Eventually there is the excitement of that first tremulous day of ownership of our very first motorcycle. Eventually we are considered to be a seasoned veteran. There are strengths and weaknesses to each of these "phases." See if the following holds true for you:

Phase I: THE PASSENGER

In this phase you have no idea of what a motorcycle is or how it works. A ride can be a pleasure, a thrill, or a Steven King-esque episode of horror, all of it dependent on the operator of the motorcycle. Most people never move on from this phase, and their opinions of motorcycles are forever etched in their minds by that first ride. In most cases, it is not a pleasant experience for them. For you, the passenger experience was either a positive, or you are so enamored of the concept that the ham-handed antics of well meaning friends or relatives were not enough to alter your course.

Phase II: THE NEOPHYTE

You have decided to become a motorcyclist. You are taking lessons from the Motorcycle Safety Foundation (please!) or, at the very least, a friend or relative who is a trusted, experienced and patient rider. You buy your first motorcycle and you ride it whenever the weather allows. The speed limit is just fine, thank you, and you are pleased when a shift sequence goes well. In order to operate the controls you have to consciously think about which is which, and what each hand or foot is doing. Wearing a helmet feels a bit weird, and you usually feel at least a little self-conscious. You are very careful when you park the bike, as you are sure it will fall over given any hint of a chance.

Phase III: THE ACCIDENT

After a few weeks or so, everything smoothes out and you begin to feel the magic. Like a person who has consumed three glasses of tequila in short order, you are invincible! Your helmet feels comfy as you float through traffic, "expertly" shifting and leaning over to feel the sides of your boots graze the tarmac. At times you laugh out loud, as you feel so one with the machine. You are sure that, if you merely willed it so, you could fly. This phase is called "The Honeymoon Glow" and it is followed, in some cases very quickly, by "The Accident."

The reason you feel so terrific is that motorcycles are wonderful machines, and you have mastered the complex skills required to operate one. At least you feel you have. You can accelerate and brake and turn, and usually at velocities that make the speed limit appear to have been set by a blind man riding a mastodon. (Actually, they are calculated for an old man in a Winnebago, so you are not far off here.) You no longer have to consciously think about which is the throttle and which the clutch. You may have even made a clutchless upshift or two, or experienced the thrill of a spinning rear tire on take-off. You have begun to explore the traction and cornering limits of your motorcycle, but in a civilized and "safe" way. This phase can last for years, if you are very lucky.

The problem is that, as impressive as your skills are, they are only of use to you when things are going well. The weather is dry, and the traffic is behaving as if controlled by logic. Except... it isn't. Chaos theory makes perfect sense to anyone who has ridden a motorcycle for a few years. Motorists will look at you, and I mean your eyes will lock with theirs; they will nod, and then promptly turn right in front of you, only to claim later that they "did not see you." Trucks will enter the road around a blind corner. There will be gravel where no gravel should logically ever accrue. You have been developing your riding talents, but not necessarily your predicting talents. Because you have been riding to safe limits in a logical world, you have little ability to react to an illogical circumstance. The result, for most of us, is an accident.

Phase IV: The Patient

Every accident will demand a recovery period, even if you emerge physically unscathed, and even if the accident was not your fault. Some would argue that every accident is to some degree your fault, because you should have been able to predict the behavior of the moron in the car that hit you, but I find that to be simplistic. Here are two examples.

My first accident was entirely my fault. I had been riding for two years and eight thousand miles. I thought I was pretty cool! I had ridden from Minneapolis to Seattle and back, which in 1968, on a Yamaha 250, was pretty special. I could ride with the best of them, I thought. Although I had experienced a few "close calls," I had never been hurt.

I celebrated my move to Seattle to begin a teaching career by tuning up my Yamaha and then barreling down a tight and winding road. It was so much fun I turned around and rode back over the same curves. I came into a corner marked 25 mph at about 65. First the pegs, dragged, and that was OK, as I was used to that; did it all of the time, in fact. Then they began to fold and my foot was scraping... I had done that lots of times, too. Then the peg bracket dragged, and jacked the rear wheel off the ground. Hadn't done that before... the result was a broken shoulder and a destroyed motorcycle. It was a very good investment in money and pain and heartache...I have not been that stupid, nor have I crashed, since that day. Let us pause to ponder, however, that tomorrow is a new day.

In example #2 I was barreling down the freeway at slightly over the speed limit, when a fellow in a van suddenly changed lines, right into the side of me. To make things worse, I had a friend on the back. The motorcycle was launched sideways at 60 mph toward an Armco barrier, and I remember looking at it and bracing for the crash. I had the bars all crossed up like a dirt tracker, and for reasons that defy my knowledge of physics to this day, I managed to sashay across four lanes of rush hour freeway in a series of lurid slides, ...without hitting anything. We ended up on the left- hand verge looking back at a black snake of a skidding tire track a few hundred feet long. The highway patrolman couldn't believe it...and neither could I. The only damage was a swollen ankle for my friend, where the bumper of the van hit him after the door curled the clutch lever rather deftly around my hand. The driver was pale with shock, and terribly apologetic. He offered to pay for my friend's x-rays, my new clutch lever, and anything else I needed. Oddly enough he had changed his mind by the time I got home.

In the first example the physical damage was severe, and took the rest of the summer to heal. In the second case I was not hurt at all, and $1.95 purchased a new clutch lever (It was a long time ago). Even so, the "incident" (not really a crash) occurred in Minneapolis on a trip, and I had to ride back to Seattle. The entire way back I became terrified whenever a vehicle was next to me on my left. I flinched at imagined lane changes, and I was uncomfortable the entire trip. When I got back to Seattle I was so shaken I put the motorcycle up for sale immediately. Fortunately, I came to my senses and changed my mind before the bike sold.

In both cases I had been injured. In the first the recovery period took several weeks and money I did not have. In the second the injuries were emotional, and it took quite some time to feel comfortable on a motorcycle again. My point would be that if you suffer through an accident, you will also need to suffer through a recovery period, even if no physical harm has come your way.

Phase V: The Motorcyclist

The way that I have arranged these "Phases" implies rather strongly that you WILL have an accident before becoming a seasoned motorcyclist. I am not sure that is true any longer with the technological capabilities built into modern motorcycles. It may now be possible to ride for years without a crash.

It is, however, a sobering thought to realize that in over three decades of riding and chatting with every motorcyclist I can meet, I have NEVER met an experienced motorcyclist who had not suffered through a crash. I am sure they're out there. At least, I hope they are. It's also possible that everyone who has been riding for years without a crash is merely locked in "Phase 2: The Neophyte," and is riding with undiluted naiveté, confident in the knowledge that nothing can possibly go awry.

In some ways, I think only an accident can get through to us the need for vigilance at all times. Motorcycles can produce such fun and such a giddy rush of euphoria that only a good solid smack on the helmet can get the point across... chaos theory is alive and well and the next exhibit is just down the road!

If you do suffer an accident, give yourself time to heal both physically and mentally, and make sure you still want to do this. Pay attention to the circumstances of the accident as well... let's not do that again!

As an experienced motorcyclist, you will be free to ride the motorcycle you have chosen in the manner you desire on the roads you have selected; fully prepared for the conditions you will meet. An experienced motorcyclist knows all about choices and consequences, and how they are the keys to true personal freedom.

CHAPTER TWELVE
Giving a Friend a First Ride

Now that you are a motorcyclist, or, if you prefer a slightly more hard-core moniker, a "biker," you will notice that ALL of your friends, co-workers, relatives, and even a surprising number of strangers, want to share their opinions. These opinions are usually not based on any degree of knowledge at all, and are, perhaps ironically, much more forcefully expressed as a result. Some will assume you are going to die in the next 24 hours, while others will be positive you are having a "mid-life crisis." Perhaps you are thought to be "going through a phase" which you will hopefully grow out of, like a teenager sporting an unfamiliar hair or clothing style. The more daring may opine, with all the subtlety of a brick through a glass window, that you are trying to compensate for a sexual dysfunction or, (slightly more palatable) choosing an accessory to match your lurid and unmentionably deviant sexual excesses.

People you know who are already motorcyclists will smile kindly and encourage you, and may offer some solace of the "been there, done that" sort as you struggle through this gauntlet of misinformation. They have probably heard exactly the same sorts of things.

Please dress your passenger as well as you would dress yourself. The preceding photo would be considered silly by any standards.

When I began motorcycling as a 20 year old, I was determined to set a good example, and to do what I could to better the group image. It took a few years to realize it was a hopeless task. I finally relaxed; when somebody made some comment about my needing a big powerful machine between my legs, I just nodded and said "that's right." This worked very well! I once had a stranger in a grocery store spot my crash helmet and say, "So, you're riding a murder-cycle, huh?" What response could I make? On the other hand...

Pause for a cute anecdote: I was 22, and on a cross-country trip on my Honda 450 Street Scrambler. Some might say this was not a suitable machine, but it was what I owned, and I had such a great time riding it on trips from Seattle to Minneapolis, Seattle to San Francisco, and Seattle to St. Petersburg, Florida (!) that I was too busy to notice I couldn't be doing it. Anyway, I stopped for a very early breakfast one Sunday morning at a truck stop cafe in rural Montana. It was a gorgeous day, and the sun beamed down on my silver and chrome machine. As I removed my helmet an elderly woman came out of the restaurant. She was obviously dressed for church, and her pleasant face spoke of a life of hard work and simple living. She strode over to me and stared at the motorcycle, and her pursed lips made me sigh internally at what was to come. She looked at me sternly and said, "My, what a beautiful motorcycle!" We had a lovely conversation, and I felt special for several days.

So, although not all will make negative comments, many cannot seem to help themselves, and they will be impervious to fact and logic. Why? Although I last studied psychology in Psych 101 in college, I think I have an idea or two.

Motorcycles are, psychologically, very basic and primeval. They combine the romance of the horse with the intrigue, danger, and distrust we feel for powerful machinery. They are also very "out there." You can be anonymous in your car driving to work, but on a motorcycle you are in peoples' faces and on their minds. Some are put off by the sheer bravado of it, and others are made to feel a bit inadequate because they could never perform such a seemingly bold and rash act. They confirm their fears and prejudices by doing what they can to make sure you are made to feel uncomfortable or less special. It is a simple thing to allow them their comfort and laugh a bit later, in the privacy of your own helmet.

Some of your friends, however, will be courageous and curious enough to ask for a ride. It is a VERY good idea to let them inquire, rather than to offer. A possible exception is in the case of a spouse, potential spouse, or life partner, where you may gently suggest such a thing. You should not, however, harp on it. Some people will never want to do go for a ride on a motorcycle, and they are probably fine human beings anyway.

More people have been turned off, for ever, by a first ride on a motorcycle than you can possibly count. The majority of motorcyclists are male, and although women are getting into the sport in rapidly increasing numbers, it is male riders who do the most damage. Male riders come equipped with testosterone, and when fueled by excitement, dramatic things can and do happen. In our enthusiasm, we often want to impress the passenger with the overwhelming performance of our machine. Thus, we take a person who has never been on a motorcycle, perch them on the back, and then subject them to acceleration and braking forces far stronger than they have ever experienced in their life, all while they are teetering unsteadily on the back of a machine they are not controlling. We may not have told them anything about how a motorcycle works, so we cast off into a sharp corner and lean the bike over, and the passenger, who has never leaned over on anything, assumes he or she is in the middle of a crash. If you are lucky, they grimly hang on to the end. If you are not, they may assume, logically, that this is going all wrong, and attempt to lean the other way. In the worst case situations, they can actually succeed in countering your efforts, and you, the passenger, and your luckless machine will all careen into the ditch. There is a much better way.

First of all, the conditions need to be right. It is a warm day, the sun is out, and nobody has consumed alcohol or anything worse. The passenger has expressed interest in a short ride, and you have a spare helmet.

When I was single I always carried a spare helmet, ensuring that I would be prepared when I met "her." Friends laughed at me...for four years. Eventually, I went to a party on my bike. I took my own six-pack... of pop, as I do not drink when I ride a bike. I met my future wife, and she was most impressed by both the pop and the spare helmet: in other words, it worked! We went out for a ride, and then dated, and then... fade to romantic music....

Begin with a short stroll around the machine, pointing out basic features: engine, brakes, turn signals, etc. You might have the person sit on the bike and explain how all of the controls work, so they will have some idea of what you will be doing. Show how the passenger pegs fold. Make sure they know where the grab handles or strap, if any, are located. Unzip the pockets of your jacket so hands can go inside them easily. Provide some simple signals, like two hits on the shoulder means, "Pull over and stop."

You need to give a short explanation of how a motorcycle corners, and instruct them to lean with you. You do not want them to be pulling against the lean, and (in rare cases) you do not want them to lean even further than you! Last, help the person put on the helmet, and do up the D rings for them.

I usually get on the motorcycle and start it before motioning for the passenger to join me. Make sure they are all set before you leave. Try to select a short route of a few miles on roads with little traffic, if at all possible, because this will be an adventure for both of you.

If you have not done this before, you may be appalled. Your finely tuned machine now seems to handle like a leaking oil tanker. What were previously surgically precise cornering lines are now uncertain lunges. It gets worse. Suddenly the braking performance has worsened appreciably. You may notice that the ride is now sloppy, and the bike wallows over bumps, apparently with a newfound and not very stable mind of its own. This is because you did not want to take the time to adjust the rear suspension for the increased load, or you forgot, or perhaps you do not know how. All of this may be made worse because you are trying so hard to be smooth and gentle, and suddenly you make awkward shifts or miss them altogether. If you hang in there for a bit, it will all work out, and your passenger will discover what a marvelous and fun machine a motorcycle can be.

I had the rare good fortune to be given my first ride, at the age of 15, by my older brother's friend. Richard was careful to do what I have now recommended, and I came back from the experience changed forever. It was literally one of the epiphanic moments of my life. I began asking my parents for a motorcycle, any motorcycle... every day. It took me five years to get one, and I never wavered. If he had been a careless clod intent on "impressing" the little kid, I might have been scared away forever, or possibly killed. Either way, I would have missed out on a passion I now know was destined to be mine forever.

Now then, if your relationship is such that subsequent rides are in the cards, you can make some gradual changes. The rear suspension can be adjusted so it is much more firm. As the passenger learns to relax, so will the death grip on your ribs. As the passenger's comfort level grows, so will yours, and soon you will be a coordinated team.

One concept that it took me 20 years to learn is the importance of discovering what kind of rides your passenger enjoys. In the early years of our marriage, I was fond of all day excursions. My wife, as I learned with glacial speed, does not care for that much of a motorcycle experience. What she does truly love is a half hour to an hour's jaunt to a sidewalk cafe. A nice lunch and a walk around and back home we go, and what a grand time we have had. She now loves motorcycling, as she defines it. She may never experience full throttle acceleration, hard braking, or the marvelous thrill of three fast downshifts and a corner attacked cleanly. She has no desire to. How I wish I had figured this out a long time ago!

There is also the possibility that you will discover that YOU do not like carrying a passenger. For many years my Yamaha 750 was set up perfectly for me. On the rare occasions when my wife went along, I was never really comfortable with the slightly more crowded seat space and the diminution in braking and handling. Besides, in the child-rearing years, it was fine to have the motorcycle be the only area of my life that was all mine, not diluted or sacrificed to the earnest needs of others. Now the children are grown, and my Kawasaki ZRX has so much horsepower it does not really notice the difference when the two of us ride together.

Besides, if you have a long-term relationship and prefer to ride alone, there is a very simple solution: a motorcycle for each of you! I'm still working on that one.

CHAPTER THIRTEEN
Commuting to Work

First of all, your boss probably won't like the idea. This is much less true these days than a few decades ago. When I was a student teacher, the principal at one high school called the University of Minnesota and demanded that the "dirty long-haired hippie" be thrown off his campus. I was certainly not dirty, my hair not long at all, and I was about as far from a hippie as a shy college student raised by parents who were both engineers and Republicans could be. What had I done?

I'd ridden my little blue and white Yamaha 250 to attend a faculty meeting and parked it in the staff parking lot. I did not have to attend the faculty meeting, and the students had left for the day, but when I walked into the room carrying my helmet under my arm I could sense the stifled gasps all around and knew I had committed a faux pas, although I couldn't imagine what it might be. Cooler heads prevailed, eventually.

When I started my first teaching year, on the other hand, the principal was happy that I rode to work. He wanted junior high students to know that you could ride a motorcycle and be a productive member of society – this as a counter to the string of less than B grade "biker" movies of the time.

Still, a motorcycle is still sufficiently out of the mainstream (c'mon, that is probably part of why you want one, you rebel you) that eyebrows may be raised. This can be possibly be eased by a couple of factors: 1.) You ARE the boss and 2.) You work for a dealership.

In all seriousness, you'll be OK, but be prepared for questions and curiosity and comments, some of them really stupid, about your new "lifestyle."

Actually riding the motorcycle to work is best covered by MSF classes and a slew of books on the topic, but there are a few "big picture" issues you might find interesting. One is flow theory.

If you take the same route to work each day, and if you work in a modern megalopolis with a lot of traffic, you'll be able to figure out which lanes on the clogged roads flow faster for each mile of your route. The right hand lane of a freeway often slows to a crawl for a mile before a popular entrance, as people merge into the right hand lane. If the next ramp is an off-ramp, conversely, the right hand lane may be the fastest.

I realize that there is a theoretical guide that drivers pick a lane according to their speed, so the left-most lane should be the fastest. I also realize that any concept of such lane-discipline went out the window a long time ago, and as long as people have cell-phones it will not return.

Time of day makes a difference. People in the morning are "pros" who do not want to be late for work. They have had coffee, or are consuming it, and they tend to be paying attention. People in the middle of the day are running errands on a route they may not know well, and are prone to sudden spasmodic lunges into a different lane. At such times of the day you will also find people driving somewhere as a part of their job. They are on the clock and in no great hurry, and may lollygaggle along with no particular attention to what is happening.

People in the evening want to get home. They want to get home now. They drive too fast, and they are tired. Some of them are suffering the effects of a "business" lunch.

The HOV lanes can help, if you have them. Do you remember what President signed a rider to a bill that allowed motorcycles to use HOV lanes? Ronald Reagan. Is that important? No. It's highly unlikely he knew it was there.

In California it's legal to "split" lanes on a motorcycle, which means you can ride in the lane between the lanes when traffic is slowed to a virtual halt. This seems insane to those of us who live in Seattle, and in many other areas, but then the California Highway Patrol "CHiPS" officers are REQUIRED to park their bikes and await a car pick-up when it rains, so clearly some different sets of priorities are at work!

A good excuse for a ride on a pleasant day when you are not at work is the researching of alternative routes. You may discover a pleasant little winding road that nobody uses, even during rush hour. It's not too likely, but hey, it's a great excuse to go for a ride or rides with a "mission"!

Overall, you must be MORE attentive when commuting to work than at any other time. And – things have gotten worse is recent years. More and more people are using cell phones all of the time, despite alarming and growing evidence that it is really not a good idea. The lust for ever larger SUVs fills the road with impenetrable tanks with smoked windows that blot out the sun – or are at least an impediment to vision. Then there are those that enjoy trimming or painting their nails, or reading the paper, or both, plus those that hide from reality with headphones powered by stereos powerful enough to provide all of the lighting for Keokuk, Iowa. Have to confess I've never been to Keokuk – I just like the name. There was once a stock car racer from Keokuk by the name of Ramo Stott, which I also remember because it is a great name. See how your mind can wander while commuting?

Why commute? Because riding a motorcycle is a joy when you want to, and why let these people take any amount of joy out of your life? Constant vigilance, the use of commuter lanes, an eye for the best route, and possible gains to be made from the use of flow theory; all can be used to make your commute a pleasure. And, you can be assured that when you arrive at work you'll be fully alert and ready to go!

CHAPTER FOURTEEN
Ten Tips

This is NOT a chapter on how to ride a motorcycle. There are many sources out there that do the job much better than I ever could, and I will let you sue them if things don't work out for you. However, there is an old adage that says "Even a blind pig finds a truffle once in awhile." To many of us, that merely raises two questions: What is a truffle? Why do I want one?

In any case, by riding motorcycles as much as possible for the past 36 years I have picked up a few ideas, concepts, and tips (truffles, perhaps?) you may find useful. Some of them you probably already know and use, but some of them tend to be "basics" that the "oldsters" forget to pass on to the "newbies" because we forget them. For your use, then, and in no particular order:

1. AVOID THE CENTER OF THE LANE. Ever notice that the center of the lane is darker? That is because it is where the old smoker of a crusty Falcon station wagon owned by the ne'er do well down to road deposits more than it's share of fossil fuels. Oil, diesel, and grease celebrate their liberation from the confines of older vehicles by painting the town black, or at least the center of the lane. This means there is less traction, and this is exacerbated wildly when it rains. If it has not rained for three weeks, it will be much worse. This is almost an argument in favor of the frequent rains in Seattle – but not quite.

2. AVOID THE PAINT. Same deal. I don't know why a culture than can put men on the moon, or develop enough nukes to turn the entire world to a glowing ember about 10,000 times (now there's a good use of technological capability), cannot seem to design a workable paint to be used for lane and intersection. The white and yellow paint used may be durable, but it is also slippery. If it gets wet, it is absolutely perilous. If you try to stop suddenly on such lines when they are wet with rain, you will crash. If you try to accelerate too hard on a longitudinal paint line running in your direction of travel, you will have a thrilling experience for sure. Been there, done that, and I still remember thinking the

clutch had exploded. Then there was the disconcerting and disorienting experience of the bike slowly rotating around on its axis, until the rear tire got to the black part and hooked up. Wow!

3. DE-MISTING. In cool or cold weather, misting up of your helmet visor can be a problem. There are various solutions and materials sold to prevent fogging, more or less. If you are fond of saving money, take some liquid dish soap and put it on a paper towel. Run it SOFTLY on the inside of the face shield, and rub it in for awhile before wiping off the excess and buffing with an old towel. This will work very well for a month or two. Then…repeat.

4. STAY COOL. Riding in hot weather can be perilous. Heat stroke is not unlikely, and it can kill you. Always carry a bandanna with you. In hot weather, stop frequently and douse it with water from the canteen you also carry with you. Tie the bandanna around your neck. The evaporation will cool you, including the major blood channels running to and from your brain. Repeat as needed. If necessary, dump water over your head and shirt. This works best if you remove your helmet and jacket first.

5. RIDE FEWER MILES IN WINTER. In some areas of the country you can ride all of the year around – or close to it. This is not true in Minnesota, and is actually one of the primary reasons why I left the day after I graduated from

college. If you are able to ride where it is cold, plan for a day with fewer hours of daylight, and plan to cover fewer miles. You will need more care, and more frequent stops. You can still have a great time; but you must accede to Mom Nature's reality or she will punish you.

6. ALWAYS CLEAN YOUR BIKE FOR SERVICE. If you do your own maintenance, you probably clean the bike before tearing into it. Imagine what life is like for a technician at a dealership. Will he or she be influenced by the condition of your bike? If the technician is human, the answer is yes. I try to have my bike as detailed as possible before allowing it to be worked on. I want them to think I am a fanatic – and I am, but the tech will not know me. (Actually, now that I work at a dealership, the techs DO know that, but I am sure you get my point.)

7. NEVER RUN OUT OF GAS. Lots of people like to brag about how far they can ride on a tank of gas. What it the world is this all about? Why? All modern bikes have either trip odometers – sometimes two – or fuel gauges, and sometimes both. Running out of gas can be dangerous, time-consuming, irritating, or all three, and it is usually totally unnecessary. Of course, I know that because I have done it. I ran out of gas in Montana, at sundown, after striking out at two towns I had mentally tagged as fuel stops. The first town had no gas station, and I had never heard of such a thing. The second

town no longer existed! Being stuck by the side of the road with a 500 pound thing of value is not a good idea.

8. BUY QUALITY. For a discussion of the concept of "quality" of extraordinary length, get yourself a copy of "Zen and the Art of Motorcycle Maintenance," by Robert Pirsig. You will read the first half of the book – about a motorcycle trip – in a day. The second half, which has the philosophy and the part about the concept of quality – took me four years to complete. Then I read it again. Then, in one of the periodic bursts of romantic idealism that periodically afflicted my teaching career, I attempted to teach the philosophic aspect of "quality" to a room of 9th graders. They surely thought me insane.

Oh yes, the point. I have made it a practice to buy only the best motorcycle gear. If I can not afford it, I wait until I can. This is the only area of my life where I have not compromised. When we were younger I bought cheap clothes, cheap food, cheap shoes, cheap cars – that was the way it had to be. But – the motorcycle was different. Everything I purchased for the bike or for me was the best I could find – when I could afford it.

It's nice to have one area of your life where you go for the top of the line – all of the time.

9. ALWAYS RIDE AT YOUR OWN PACE. Sooner or later you will have the chance to ride with others. Some of them will think they are faster than you are. Some of them are. Some of them "need" to prove this. LET THEM! There is nothing worse than riding a bike when the "red mist" falls, and attempting to ride over your head. This is particularly a problem with sport bikes. Yes, I have done it, I'm sorry to say. On more than one occasion I found myself "chasing" a friend who was on a better and faster bike – and this will surely lead to disaster. As an Australian mate said "David, let the puppies go." He was right. You will be better off, and they will usually get the tickets!

10. NEVER RIDE ANGRY. Motorcycles are NOT a good way to "show them." We all have bad days when we would like to tell off the boss, or the wife, and it may me tempting to take out our rage on the poor motorcycle. This is a bad idea! You need to calm down and go back to the mantra: "When the helmet drops, the bullshit stops."

Explanatory anecdote: In college I became engaged, briefly, to the girl of my dreams. She decided we were too young to be married. She was right, and MaryLee, wherever you are, thank you from the bottom of my heart. During the latter stages of our relationship, before the final catastrophe, we had some sort of argument on the phone. I stormed out of my rental house, fueled to the max with raging hormones and testosterone, and hopped on my bike.

We rocketed down the alleyway with a scream of 250 snarling ccs that truly alarmed my housemates. I rode like a total idiot for about 5 miles, braking late, cornering hard, accelerating with all of the gusto the little bike could muster. Gradually, it began to dawn on me. I had wanted a bike, this bike, for every day of a long five years. I had known MaryLee for one year. If I blew up the bike, I could never replace it. I would surely never know love again (insert lovelorn sigh), but I would have my bike. I rode it back to the house, meekly, and I have never ridden angry since.

CHAPTER FIFTEEN
How to Talk Motorcycle

The dictionary of terms that follows is not meant to be complete, but will give you a smattering of vocabulary to either talk with experienced motorcyclists, or to have some notion of what in the world they are talking about!

AJS: ancient British brand of motorcycle, long defunct and therefore glorified beyond all reason. (Such is true of virtually all British motorcycle brands)

ABS: automated braking systems. Similar to that used on many cars, but much more of an engineering challenge. First debuted by Yamaha, and now common on large touring bikes and some sport models. Some traditionalists still grumble about a loss of feel and rider input – but the advantages of being able to stop quickly on gravel or ice(!) are gradually winning over the masses.

Aprilia: Italian manufacturer showing impressive machinery and rapid growth.

Beater-bike: term for a motorcycle that appears to be trashed. Some prefer this look as an anti-style statement. A beater-bike may be in sound mechanical condition, but most are exactly what they appear to be. Buying one would be an exercise is masochism.

Bias-ply: up until recently, type of construction used in all motorcycle tires, referring to the angle to the tread of the supporting belts in the tire carcass. Now supplanted by tubeless radial tires.

Bikini: No, not what you want your comely passenger to wear! This is a fairing type, one that covers only the headlight and instruments. Made popular by the BMW R90S of the late 60s, and a staple of the cafe racer "look." Also referred to as a 1/4 fairing.

Bimota: exclusive Italian cottage industry motorcycle powered by a variety of Italian or Japanese engines. Exquisite fit and finish, and often blur the distinction between transportation and art.

BMW: Bavarian Motor Werkes, or Bayerische Motor Werkes. Same German folks who bring you the delectable cars.

Bob-job: see Chopper

BSA: see AJS

Buell: Sporting range of Harleys. Led by innovative design by Eric Buell, and now a strong player in area of sports motorcycles. Some reliability and build quality questions have now been addressed and Buell is an exciting brand today, even launching into the perilous waters of "first bike" models.

Cafe racer: term coined in the 60s in Europe for a bike altered in appearance to resemble a road racer. Used to "race" from cafe to cafe. Had a brief spurt of popularity in the 70s in America, and has now been subsumed by radical racer replica models from all manufacturers. Both will feature lowered handlebars and raised and rear set foot pegs for a posture ideal for hard and fast winding roads, but anatomically excruciating for any extended period of riding in the real world. Still a stylish way to go.

Cagiva: Italian motorcycle manufacturer. Formerly one with Ducati, but now a separate entity.

Can: slang term for an aftermarket replacement muffler. Will usually be lighter than the stock system, almost always louder, and mayor may not improve performance.

Chaps: leather pants made to be worn over jeans. As such they will have zippers down the side and a crotchless design to make them easy to don. Some folks love them, while others cannot imagine wearing them and keeping a straight face. Very handy if you ever need to do your Village People impersonation!

Chopper: original "bad boy" version of a Harley, a style begun post-war by GIs "chopping" off extraneous parts of a stock Harley to create a lighter, lower, and faster machine. Also known as a "bob job." Choppers are often modified in the direction of a moving work of art, and sometimes the designers lose track of the original purpose of a motorcycle. A well-done chopper is a wonderful thing, and also somewhat rare.

Clone: a motorcycle styled and or designed to resemble a top-selling design from as different manufacturer, as in millions of Japanese clones of Harley-Davidson models.

Cruiser: any motorcycle styled and designed to be used for casual and friendly rides. Usually will feature a laid-back riding position and forward pegs. Modern cruisers feature lots of torque, and chrome embellishments running from the showy to the excessive.

Desmodromic: type of valve actuation, favored by Ducati, utilizing small auxiliary springs. Originally gave a technological advantage at the cost of complexity, now used as a marketing advantage that screams "European sophistication," but offers no advantage at all, other than the complexity loved by many.

Excelsior: storied American brand, now defunct. Recent revival with the addition of Henderson, another storied American name, and now both are defunct ...again. Sigh.

Fairing: a combination of a windshield and bodywork in various degrees of coverage. In general, a bikini, or 1/4 fairing, covers the headlight and instruments, a 1/2 fairing extends further down to encase the top half of the engine, and a full fairing covers the entire engine.

Feathering: either the light application of throttle, as in "feathering the throttle" or the gentle fraying of the tire at the very edge of the tread when riders get down to the last fraction of available traction. "Squids" have been known to use a file to hand-feather their tires so that they look like the bike is ridden more aggressively than the rider's talent will allow.

FUBAR: acronym for "fouled up beyond all repair," although the f can be replaced by a stronger term. Similar to SNAFU.

Gentleman's Express: 70s term for a cafe racer made utile. A Gentleman's Express should have a good turn of speed and a reasonably aggressive riding stance, but also comfort and some storage capacity. This term has now been replaced by the much less elegantly phrased but also non-sexist "Sports Tourer." A pity.

Greeves: see AJS

Harley-Davidson: THE American motorcycle. Almost went belly up in the 70's and suffered through several years as a subsidiary of AMF (known for their bowling balls). An extremely ballsy management buyout in 1980 looks like sheer genius today, as they bound from strength to strength. Harleys are (usually) very expensive and not very fast, nor do they handle or brake especially well, but no other brand offers a sound and spirit that resonates so well in the American psyche.

Honda: the biggest of the Japanese big 4, and the biggest, by far, in the world. Begun by Soichiro Honda melting down pots and pans to create tiny engines to bolt onto bike frames in occupied Japan. Mr. Honda was the first to build reliable and inexpensive motorcycles, and he alone is responsible for motorcycling as it is today. Probably one of the most important human beings in any endeavor anywhere, ever.

Indian: At one time much larger than Harley-Davidson, and the dominant American brand. Management glommed onto huge military contracts in WWI and ignored their civilian customer base. When the war went away they had lost much of their civilian base, and could not recover. Three decades of management bungles followed, matched only by the British industry in the 60s (see AJS) until the last Indian tottered off the line in 1953. A famous name that died, was battled over in court for twenty years, and now a viable brand again.

Isle of Man: the last "real" road race in the world. Held over a 37 mile long course on a small island, Tourist Trophy entrants blast through small British villages on quaint (narrow) roads, past curbs and over manhole covers and up and down a mountain at breathtaking and occasionally fatal speeds. If I sell enough of these books I hope to go there!

Kawasaki: one of the Japanese big 4 manufacturers.

Laverda: Italian synonym for "see AJS." But! About to be relaunched by Aprilia - maybe.

Linked brakes: system of connecting the rear and front brakes for a more even distribution of braking load. Favored by Honda and Moto-Guzzi on some models, offers some advantages but also some disadvantages, since there are times when you might only wish to apply the rear brake.

Luggage rack: rack mounted above the rear fender and behind the seat to carry more stuff. Modern sports bikes with swoopy and aerodynamic plastic body panels make for a design challenge, while larger and larger touring bikes have racks capable of supporting a small town.

Mandarin: type of collar on many leather jackets with a flap that snaps across the throat area.

Mono-shock: any rear suspension design using only one shock absorber instead of two. Can be connected to various linkages to alter the shocks performance, and serves to narrow the rear of the motorcycle.

Moto-Guzzi: storied Italian manufacturer known for large V twins and prodigious amounts of torque. At first ride you will think they are crazy, but a Moto-Guzzi will quickly grow on you. A very different set of design answers to common questions.

MSF: Motorcycle Safety Foundation. Offers beginner and experienced rider courses in your area, and you need to sign up for one today. The best single investment you can make in motorcycling enjoyment and long-term safety. An absolute must.

Naked: currently in-vogue styling trend for a powerful sport bike with little or no bodywork. Creates something of the look of a UJM from the 70s, albeit with vastly increased horsepower. Usually offers a more upright riding position as well. Typically has less extreme performance than a sports bike, in a trade-off for ease of use and a broader span of possible uses, and may, as in the Kawasaki ZRX, carry forth styling clues from classic factory road racers of a particular era.

Nitrous oxide: forced induction system in which doubly oxygenated air is injected into the fuel stream, allowing far more fuel to be burned. Creates drastic increases in horsepower and, unless carefully engineered, equally drastic and usually explosive engine failures.

Norton: See AJS, but also one of the most storied names in motorcycling. Still ridden and loved by thousands, even though production ceased in the 70's. Attempts at revivals for twenty years have been tragicomic or disastrous, and usually both, but now things appear to be stable with new Nortons coming on-line from Kenny Dreer in Oregon - Norton is now a USA motorcycle!

Polaris: Canadian manufacturer, originally of snowmobiles, and now having some success with large tourers and sport-tourers.

Rear-sets: aftermarket apparatus used to locate the footpegs, shift lever, and rear brake lever higher and more to the rear. This will increase the ground clearance, at the expense of a more drastically contorted riding position. Usually found on sport bikes, which already have a lot of ground clearance, for that "racy" look. There is no modern street motorcycle that "needs" these, but they are cool to many. They can be added to good functional effect on some older classic designs.

Royal Enfield: see AJS

Saddlebags: wonderful term from the days when horsepower was a literal term. Bags that fit on either side of the rear of the seat. "Soft" models are some sort of woven materials, and "hard" bags are usually fiberglass. Leather models often resemble designs from over a century ago.

Skunk works: slang term for any manufacturer's private research and development lab, where strange and unimaginable delights are created, or at least we like to hope so.

SNAFU: acronym for "Situation Normal, All Fouled Up," although once again the F is often replaced with a stronger term. See FUBAR.

Sports tourer: see Gentleman's Express

Spring rider: sarcastic term for an overly enthusiastic rider of great ego and little skill who prefers to go fast right now and learn the hard way. May not be alive by fall.

SQUID: generic term for a moron who gives all a bad name. Usually a young man in cut-offs and tennis shoes riding a very loud motorcycle far too fast in the wrong places. See "spring rider." May actually mean "Surely Quicker Until I Die."

Sunbeam: see AJS

Superbike: a definition that changes each year - the latest and greatest and fastest machine available. Technological innovation keeps moving the bar upward on this one, so today's superbike becomes tomorrow's sport bike. Hard to imagine that anyone needs 170 hp and a top speed of 200 mph. On the other hand, the Honda 4 of 1969 is generally considered to be the first superbike, and at the time four cylinders and 75 horsepower was considered to be over the top... and it was.

Suzuki: one of the Japanese big 4 manufacturers.

Tank bag: as the name suggests, a bag that attaches to the... tank! Common and very useful accessory offered by many manufacturers, either with some sort of harness or magnets as the attachment system.

Telescopic: front fork design used on almost all current motorcycles, where a sliding shaft telescopes in and out of a holder. Not an elegant or brilliant solution perhaps, but still better than other solutions over a wide range of surfaces.

Top trunk: typically a fiberglass trunk to mount on a luggage rack behind the seat. May be designed to work in conjunction with a set of saddlebags.

Tourer: large motorcycle designed for trips across states and possibly countries, or at least the appearance of that capability. May feature stereos that adjust volume with speed, trip computers, CB radios, GPS, and all sorts of other techno- wizardry. Some are now so vast they require a reverse gear to back up, and may begin to blur the line between motorcycle and car. On the other hand, nothing is as comfortable for a long journey, most especially if you travel as a couple. Most are supported by rabidly enthusiastic clubs. You do not have to have matching jackets and helmets and a stuffed toy mounted on the luggage rack, but everyone else will sport such finery.

Triumph: almost a "see AJS", but has been brought back by John Bloor over the past twenty years. Idiosyncratic line of utterly beautiful motorcycles. Anyone with a soul has to root for their continued success. Now beginning to take on the Japanese giants.

Trochoidal: type of oil pump in a Yamaha triple. You have no need to know this; I just think it is a fabulous word!

Turbocharging: uses the rush of exhaust gases to spin a turbine wheel connected to a second turbine wheel that forces more air into the engine. Can create much more horsepower, at the expense of increased complexity and cost and potentially, at least, reduced reliability.

UJM: Universal Japanese Motorcycle. Handy acronym to describe a Japanese motorcycle with a transverse 4 cylinder engine. The Honda 750 4 of 1969 is the grandfather that spawned several million descendants...many of them excellent.

USD: Upside down forks. Most motorcycles have a front suspension consisting of telescopic tubes, or "forks." The slider tube is called the "male slider" and the larger hollow tube it slides in is called the "female." No points for figuring out the history of these terms.

For fifty years, the heavier "female" tube was mounted at the bottom, and the "male" slider plunged up and down into the female tube – getting sweaty, isn't it?

In recent years "USD" or "upside down" forks have been developed. In these the er, um…, positions, are reversed, with the female on top. This has some advantages (ask any woman – sorry – I could not resist) in terms of (oh Lord!) stiffness and rigidity.

Who knew that writing a dictionary could be such an exciting experience? Melville Dewey, for one – who invented the Dewey Decimal System used by all modern libraries – but that is a long story for a different book!

Velocette: see AJS

WFO: Ancient acronym used in motorcycle tall tales that frequently end in disaster -refers to the throttle as being Wide F***ing Open!

Wheelie bars: used on drag bikes. Small wheels at the end of spring steel struts jutting out behind the bike several feet to keep it from flipping over backwards under impossibly rapid acceleration.

Yamaha: one of the Japanese big 4 companies, also known much longer for their musical instruments. Their first US models featured the corporate logo on the side of the crankcase…three crossed tuning forks. Some of their current models are returning to this emblem, which is pretty cool to the people who know what it represents – and now you are one of them.

CHAPTER SIXTEEN
Cleanliness is Next to Godliness

Well, close anyway. There are a great many things to be said for keeping your motorcycle clean. The time spent on this task can be a pleasant break from the cares of the day or, best of all, a great way to finish a day's ride. The physical act of cleaning the bike will force you to look at it carefully, allowing even the most mechanically myopic to spot something that is going amiss, so your safety is enhanced. Last but not least, you look better riding on a clean bike!

As usual, even such a simple task as washing a

motorcycle requires some thought. We are separating "cleaning" here from "detailing," or "restoring." There are entire books written on those topics, and this is not one of them. However, "Motorcycle Restoration 101," by Tom Mehren, IS one of them – end of shameless plug.

My preferred time to clean the bike is when I get home from a ride of a goodly length, or when I have been riding in the rain, or when there is a professional stick and ball game on the radio to provide the correct ambience to my driveway. I have heard that some folks actually spend large amounts of money to attend these games in person, for reasons that elude me.

Anyway, the first step, if the bike is still warm and it has chain drive, is to lubricate the chain. Spray-on chain lubes have two ingredients – light oil and a heavier lubricant. The light oil is there to carry the lube out of the spray nozzle and onto the chain – and it is this light oil that does most of the splattering. If you spray the chain while it is still hot, the light oil will evaporate, and the heavier lube will have a better chance to penetrate. If you have a Harley with belt drive or a shaft drive bike, you can skip this step and the next one, nod your head, smile at the folly of the rest of us, and proceed.

The next step is for those who like a clean rear wheel. A little WD40 on a rag will clean off the chain lube overspray and spatter and assorted other gunk on the rear wheel and chain guard.

After that it gets pretty easy. You spray down the bike with a hose, using some care to not direct a stiletto stream into the air intakes or the exhausts (…and just why would anyone do that?) and get the bike good and wet. Soap and your favorite sponge or mitt or whatever goes in a pail with more water. You can buy special soaps that are a little softer if you are worried about scratching the paint, although I used hand dish soap for decades with no problems to speak of. Like a car, you want to start from the top and work down, use a lot of water, and rinse frequently.

When you're done, spray down the entire bike again. Then remove the nozzle from the hose and do it one last time, this time using the running water stream to "sheet" as much of the water off as possible. Now you are ready to spend as much time as you want with a beverage of choice, perhaps a pipe or a cigar, and some towels you rescued when your wife had to replace all the linens because the relatives you don't like anyway were coming for Christmas and we did not want them to think we had no taste. Actually, you kind of DID want to make them think you had no taste, but you kept quiet, and the old towels are your reward for tact.

All dry? If time remains, go ahead and wax the bike – it won't take that long. Or it can, if you're having fun and want it to. There are now hundreds of waxing products available. The expensive ones do seem to do a better job but again, for decades I used whatever was on sale.

Once you are all done, or decide to move on to another task, run the bike for a minute or two to heat up and evaporate any water down in the nooks and crannies. Presto – your bike looks fabulous in the garage and is ready for the next adventure.

CHAPTER SEVENTEEN
The Long Trip

Once you own a bike, the lure of the open road will enter your life. In fact, the odds are that you thought about this for quite some time before you even owned a motorcycle. Perhaps you never mentioned it to anyone else, and it may have even seemed silly at times, but yet...

There are good reasons why many ads on TV for motorcycles and other products feature a lone rider motoring across an endless and gorgeous landscape. They work because the rider on the long trip is a very romantic and powerful image to attach to your product. Of course, such an image also works well when attached to you.

Far from being a silly affectation, a motorcycle trip can do many good things for you that will last for months and even decades upon your return. Such a trip can enhance self-confidence, lower blood pressure, and provide priceless time for thought and self-reflection. Of course, it can also kill you, so a bit of planning would not go amiss.

You first need to determine where you want to go and how long you will need to get there. By all means estimate for more miles than you think are going to be involved, and calculate your trip for fewer miles per day than you would in a car.

I know, I know, a motorcycle is SO much faster! But it also requires more concentration, and takes a lot more out of you. The essential difference is that in a car you are driving to get to somewhere fun, and on a motorcycle the fun is to be had in the getting there. Therefore, plan in advance to make the ride the fun part. The destination can approach irrelevance. In fact, some plan to avoid…planning. Some motorcyclists are able to enjoy trips with no destination at all, but most of us need some point at which to arrive, just to keep those remaining shards of Type A personality at peace within.

First of all, we need to narrow down a tad the definition of "trip." We are not too worried about the number of days, in this case, but with the definition of how the days are to be spent. At one extreme you can hit the Interstate system aboard a luxury tourer, make lodging reservations on the fly with your cell phone, pause only for fuel and the obligatory purchase of a new CD or two about every other state, and cover truly massive distances in relative comfort. At the other end you take the 1972 Yamaha 350 you purchased from that nice man down the street who had not ridden it in a score of years, bungie your duffle on the seat and take off, roaming at will the smallest highways of your area. You might cover only 150 miles per day, and who is to say had the grander time?

For this book we will work from a base of the kind of trips I like to take (hey, I'm writing it!) and you can modify to taste. For most of my trips, I use a large sport bike, and I camp out most of the time. Motels are reserved for a truly awful rain system that appears determined to stick with me, or, on a longer trip, the occasional sybaritic excess of a good bed and a hot shower, etc. I try to avoid the Interstate system whenever possible, sticking to two lane state highways. You can get almost anywhere in the United States on state routes, with less traffic and more scenery. I usually go from 450 - 600 miles a day if traveling by myself, and at least 100 miles less if with a friend of two.

To be, or not to be, two... or more

Ah yes, the matter of who shall go? I have assumed here that you will be riding alone on the bike, because the market for this book is meant to be motorcyclists new to the experience. There are lots of folks who travel two up, usually on large touring bikes, but most neophytes will be happier riding solo. Of course, Susan and I did take our honeymoon on a motorcycle... a Honda 500-4 (!), in March on the Washington and Oregon coasts (!!), and it did not rain (!!!), but then again, we only covered some 500 miles in 5 days.

If riding solo, is it best to go with a friend or alone? Depends on you, and depends on the friend. It is MUCH safer, in most cases, to ride with a friend. There is strength in numbers, and solace in mechanical mishap. I will accept feminist outrage, if any, by recommending that any woman on a trip should not ride alone. I know all about equality, and she can do anything I can do, and yadayadaya, but there are some men who do not react well to the sight of a woman alone on a motorcycle. Enough said? Probably not, but that's all that will be said.

There are some drawbacks to riding with a friend or two to be considered. The motorcycles need to be fueled more often, and it takes <u>much</u> longer to do anything. You need to have a common understanding about appropriate speeds, places to stop, when to sightsee, etc. On one horrid five day leg of an otherwise great trip, I learned that one of the most important factors to be ironed out, BEFORE you leave, is when to start and when to stop. I prefer to get going as early as possible (the light just after dawn is gorgeous) and to stop in the early evening or even late afternoon, as I love hanging around a camp at the end of a good day. My mid-trip acquaintance preferred to ride from about 10 AM to 10 PM. We were lucky nobody was killed in the ensuing week of psychic struggle!

It's amazing what small details will require thought and discussion. What is a good touring speed, for example? 65? 72? 95? What side of the lane do you prefer, out by the center stripe or in by the curbside? And who leads?

Here are some answers to try on for psychic size:

SPEED

Most motorcycles seem to have a "sweet spot" for touring, a speed and rpm range where all of the mechanical parts seem to be humming along in jolly synchronicity. Usually this is a figment of your mind, however, and you can easily go 5 mph faster or slower and the bike will not care. Therefore, the chosen speed should be set by the person in front.

LANES

In the preceding chapter we covered the idea of avoiding the very center of the lane. Now the question becomes – right or left side? I prefer the outer part of the lane (left in this country), so I have the widest margin of error on either side of the bike, and the best sight lines into oncoming corners. Some prefer the inside, further away from both oncoming traffic and anyone passing on the left. There are probably many more sound arguments in favor of one or the other, but the one you are most comfortable with is probably best for you.

LEADER

Do you want to be the bike in front? There is usually not one answer to this question. It depends on who you are riding with, and on what sort of roads. If you take several trips with the same people, you will gradually learn what kind of riding each prefers on what kind of road. There is a special inner satisfaction about riding with a friend and communicating with hand signals, nods of the head, and sometimes nothing at all – you just know what will work in a given situation. The point is that there is MUCH more to touring than simply riding your motorcycle, and you and any riding partners need to work out as many of these concepts as you can in advance.

Keeping an open mind and being flexible will make things work well.

KEEPING AN OPEN MIND

One of the hardest things to do is adjust to the thinking and traveling pace of a motorcycle. We are so used to following schedules and being task-oriented in our daily lives that it can be a real feat to mentally toss all agendas out the side of your helmet. However, the rewards are well worth it in terms of memories and fun.

An adventure for me was traveling all of the way across Montana on small highways, determining my route by gazing ahead to see where the rain clouds would be... something you can do quite easily in "Big Sky" country. I used this system to ride from Seattle to Georgia without ever getting wet, and along the way I visited many small towns I might have missed if droning along in a downpour on the Interstate.

A friend's little technique is to start thinking about a campground at about 4 in the afternoon, and he carries a book with him of little and obscure campgrounds. I thought this was truly insane until two or three years went by with no trouble finding a camp site.

I do think it's a wonderful idea to plan your trip in advance. I spend many a comfortable evening huddled over my road atlas mentally planning routes and schedules, and I do this for months before the actual trip. However, once the trip starts, alterations will begin almost immediately, and you need to be able to embrace them!

One of the real advantages with traveling with a friend or two comes at mealtime. First of all, you are having a grand adventure, and there is much to be shared in what happened on the road since the last stop. In addition, when traveling by myself, I tend to order a meal and then eat it and go, since there is not conversation taking place. I cover more ground in a day, but have less fun.

HOW TO EAT ON A TRIP

Again, this is what works for me. Get up and get going, fairly early. Assuming this is a summer trip, there is hardly anything more beautiful than the roads, almost anywhere in this country, in the early morning light. After a few miles, reward yourself with a stop at a roadside cafe, probably one with several semis parked around it. Order a ham and cheese omelet and toast and coffee. You will probably be served enough food to keep a God-fearing and homophobic Boy Scout troop energized on a 15 mile hike. Once fed, or rather, stuffed, you can go the rest of the day with a snack here or there.

ALWAYS carry water and a candy bar or whatever on the bike, just in case.
Dinner can be a problem when camping, as cooking gear takes up a lot of room. If you do not want to carry the utensils, stove, etc., there is a simpler method. Find a campground within ten miles of a town, which is easy, as most of them are. Set up your tent. Ride into town, with now empty saddle bags. Most grocery stores now have a deli section with all sorts of mouth-watering sandwiches. Buy some sandwiches, chips, cookies, the evening paper, a motorcycle magazine and some paper towels. Put them in one saddlebag. Buy a bag of ice and some milk, pop, and

whatever other beverages you desire. Put them in the other bag. When you arrive back at camp you will have dinner, some evening reading, and chilled beverages! No plates, no stove, and no clean-up.

Although not a big drinker, I find that a beer or two or a small glass of scotch helps me turn off the laser-eyed concentration I have been using all day on the bike. You have to give your body a signal that it is OK to turn off the adrenaline pump, or you will never get to sleep! The ice in the saddlebag will probably last until morning, and the last swig of chilled milk and a cookie will get me up and running, and provide sustenance until I find that truck stop for the omelet breakfast!

CHAPTER EIGHTEEN
Caveats

Every book ever written is chock full of the biases of the author, whether he or she knew they were there or not. Here are some of mine – obviously the ones I am aware of.

WHERE I WORK

I work for a Cycle Barn. Having spent 31 years toiling in the trenches teaching teens the tenuous joys of our language, (not to mention alliteration) I am enjoying a second career as part of the management team of the largest motorsports dealership in Washington and several other states.

Due to this, you may notice a bias in favor of shopping for your motorcycle needs at a dealership. In my defense, I had the same bias for the thirty years when I was a motorcyclist but not a dealership employee. I always wanted to see exactly what I was buying, and since motorcycle items are very personal, this made some sense, and still does.

The rest of my bias comes from a somewhat romantic personal philosophy. I am a person who likes the art of Norman Rockwell. I believe that everything you need to know about life is contained in the play "Our Town, by Thornton Wilder. For what I have learned from works like this, I have always endeavored to spend my money in the same community where it is earned.

WHAT I RIDE

On the one hand, I get to ride everything as a part of my job at Cycle Barn. I now have notes on 160 different motorcycles, and counting. Now there would be a fun read! Although I tend to find something to like in every bike I ride, with about five exceptions, all experienced motorcyclists have a favorite "niche" that slants their view of motorcycle design. In my case, that is sport bikes and naked sport bikes. That is reflected in my garage, which often houses a bike I am riding for Cycle Barn, but always has my two favorite bikes – the two I own. I have a 1999 Kawasaki ZRX, which is a naked sport bike, and a 2000 Kawasaki ZX12R, which is one of the fastest sport bikes ever built.

I have no particular favoritism for Kawasaki, as might reasonably be inferred – that is just the way things are at this time. In the past I have owned Hondas (3), Yamahas (2), a third Kawasaki, and a Norton, and I may own a few other brands in the future, and they will likely be of a sporting bent.

WHAT I LEARNED FROM JAMES BOND

No, not the movies. When I was a pubescent teen I read all of Ian Fleming's books on James Bond, and they left a lasting impact on what I want and how I approach the world.

Of course, at that age what I wanted was to have scads of gorgeous women become breathless at the very sight of me, and plot how they could be favored with my tremendous love-making skills. Alas, I never developed the "knack," and what a relief! Imagine the voice messages and e-mails a James Bond would get every day – you'd never get anything done!

What I did take from the books was James Bond's incredible eye for detail. In situation piled on circumstance, in chapter after incident, he would pick up some detail from his surroundings that would help him solve the crime, avoid the assassin, and bed the girl.

By the time I completed the Bond novels I was in college, and I would "practice" on my way to class. I noticed that the wrought iron railings in the lecture hall were actually spectacularly beautiful, and marveled that nobody else noticed them. I sat in front of the Greek columns of a lecture hall one night in a big snowstorm and created some truly wonderful poetry – at least it seemed wonderful at the time, as I did not write it down and could never remember it later. Did you know that Robert Palmer dreamed the song "Addicted to Love" and the video that went with it? He woke up and wrote it down, and then went back to sleep. That is why he is rich and I am not…. Or maybe not.

Ironically, my attention to detail was practice for the motorcycle I was soon to buy, for on a motorcycle it is the ability to notice detail that is your best friend. You will notice the tire going flat on the car in front, before it lurches into your lane. You will be able to deduce the actions of others based merely on their facial expression, or the physical attitude of their car. You will be perceptive to minute changes in air pressure, able to detect a loss of as much as one pound in a rear tire. You can detect minute changes in sound caused by another bike or vehicle close to you, and you can "feel" the presence of another bike in a corner, even though you cannot see it. Riding by the seat of your pants is very real, and can be learned.

If you already have this talent, then you noticed that the Table of Contents advised the reader to look at this chapter first – and you did. Now you can nod sagely, smile a Bondian grin, and go about the business of riding motorcycles. If not – practice, practice, practice!

Ride safe, ride fast, and ride often.